The Best of
Waterfront View

The Best of

Waterfront View

By Vic Dunaway

WICKSTROM
PUBLISHERS, INCORPORATED
5901 SW 74th STREET, MIAMI, FLORIDA 33143

Other Books by Vic Dunaway

Complete Book of Baits, Rigs and Tackle
From Hook to Table
Modern Saltwater Fishing

Library of Congress Catalog Card Number: 88-51540

Copyright © 1989 by Wickstrom Publishers Inc.

Printed in the United States of America

ISBN 0-936240-05-9   ISBN 0-936240-03-2 (pbk.)

About This Book

Sweets to Savor

Like a big box of juicy chocolates, this special collection of columns by Vic Dunaway is sure to tickle the sweet tooth of your brain.

Vic's extraordinary sense of humor gives you round after round of deep-down amusement, punctuated by out-loud laughs that will brighten your days, over and over.

It's no wonder that famous writer Frank Sargeant calls Vic "The dean of outdoor humorists," although Vic himself would be the last to claim such a title.

For more than a decade, Dunaway's "Waterfront View" column has led off the content in *Florida Sportsman* Magazine. His writings attracted numerous awards from judges. More importantly, his hilarious stories win constant praise and adulation from the magazine's readership.

This one-of-a-kind collector's volume brings together 78 memorable columns. "The Best of Waterfront View" is fun for all, and if you're an outdoors person, the book is an absolute must.

Take one or two columns a day for what ails you, or maybe at bedtime in order to end your day with a smile.

It's our pleasure to pass to you this bountiful box of sweets. Enjoy them all, one by one.

Karl Wickstrom, Publisher
Florida Sportsman Magazine

The Best of

Waterfront View

By Vic Dunaway

TABLE OF CONTENTS

7

9

The Angling Gourmet

As every fisherman knows, there are established and accepted ways of doing things, and if you breach certain hallowed traditions you are subject to harsh criticism by your peers.

One of those inviolable traditions is the fisherman's luncheon. The list of menu items is firmly fixed. No veteran angler worthy of the name has strayed from it in all his career, and a novice who unwittingly substitutes other provender risks instant shame.

As a service to the uninitiated, the full and complete list of authorized recipes follows:

APPETIZERS: Potato chips, corn chips and cheese puffs are all acceptable. To serve, place ripped-open bags of them on casting deck and console. Run boat briskly for several minutes. This distributes the appetizers so they are in convenient reach of fishermen in various corners of the boat, who locate them easily by the crunching sounds underfoot.

VIENNA SAUSAGE: Remove lid from can and drain liquid overside, taking care that it does not come in contact with boat hull, as it may dissolve aluminum or gelcoat. Use brace and bit or corkscrew to remove first sausage from can. Discard. Remaining sausages may be served to those aboard who have taken Dramamine.

BOLOGNA SANDWICHES: For each sandwich, take two slices of bread from boat's dry-storage compartment. Squeeze gently until water no longer drips. Spread between two slices of bologna.

COLD FRIED CHICKEN: Pick up chicken at neighborhood franchise the day before trip. To serve, scrape coating from chicken and reserve for patching cracks in fiberglass. Chicken may be eaten with the fingers. Fingers may be cleaned with mineral spirits and a coarse file.

SARDINES: Open can as far as possible (approximately one-eighth inch) with key or tool provided. Continue opening with ice pick and pocket knife. Complete opening with screwdriver, hammer and pliers.

Wipe blood from hands before serving.

CHEESE AND CRACKERS: Cut slices of processed American cheese into quarters. Place each quarter on a soda cracker and top with a second cracker.

If processed American cheese is not available, a third cracker may be substituted without affecting flavor.

POTTED MEAT: Open can with label facing you, so as to avoid accidentally reading list of ingredients on back. Dip meat from can with crackers or chips.

Leftover potted meat may be stored in the refrigerator and used as buzzard repellent.

DESSERT: The only acceptable angler's dessert is a chocolate bar. May be eaten with plastic spoon or soda straw, or licked directly from the wrapper.

Who Thinks Like a Fish?

Anyone who brings home fish with moderate consistency may one day hear it said of himself that he "thinks like a fish." He will consider it a great compliment, but it is really an insult. The thoughts of fish are neither brilliant nor profuse.

Fish, as a matter of fact, think only four thoughts in all their lives. They think they would like to be comfortable. They think they would like to have something to eat. They think they would like to escape the clutches of would-be predators. They think they would like to spawn.

It's a sad human indeed who can't think those same four thoughts more lucidly, and certainly more frequently, than a fish.

The intelligence of fish is a myth created by the unsuccessful fisherman. Take, for example, the common case of a school of snapper in clear water under a dock. They hungrily gobble up any free-sinking tidbits tossed to them, but ignore the same delicacies when borne into their midst by hook, line and half-ounce sinker.

"Boy!" exclaims the astonished fisherman. "Are those snapper ever *smart!*"

To impress that same guy with your own intelligence, you'd need only send back your steak in a fancy restaurant because it has a rusty hook stuck in the middle of it, and a kinky scraggle of monofilament tracing a path across the mashed potatoes over to where an egg sinker garnishes the asparagus in hollandaise sauce.

Or let's say you are crossing a four-lane highway. You suddenly notice a Mack truck bearing down upon you at 60 miles per hour, its operator oblivious to your presence because he is caught up in pre-spawn behavior, waving at a passing blonde in a convertible.

You run for your life, barely reaching the safety of the sidewalk. As you stand there huffing and puffing, are you besieged by Rhodes scholars eager to heap praise upon your intelligence? Of course not. Yet the equivalent action of a bonefish earns the accolades of anglers everywhere.

What happens is that the bonefish glances up from his bottom-grubbing to see, looming near, the refracted squiggles of an 18-foot boat, topped by two-legged monsters gesturing menacingly at him with long sticks. The bonefish skeedaddles. The anglers marvel at his brilliance.

A bass fisherman spends an hour trying to convince a pot-bellied Mama bass on her bed that she should swallow an eight-inch plastic lizard with purple spots and a red tail. Finally he gives up and pronounces the fish "too smart." It does not occur to him that she is thinking about something besides dining.

Again, trying to place that experience in understandable human perspective, let us ponder what might happen if the angler's own wife were lying in bed, preened and perfumed, and he stalked silently to the bedroom door and tossed a wiggly, purple-spotted, red-tailed plastic lizard right on top of her peignoir.

Unlike a fish, she would think many more thoughts than four, none of them printable here.

Three Famous Stories

Probably you know that newspapers keep on hand ready-written obituaries of famous living persons, so that when one of them thoughtlessly dies five minutes before press time, the story can be rushed into print.

I have long suspected that they do much the same thing with fishing features—not the outdoors columns, of course, but those cutesy little pieces which, with only minor changes such as names and locale, they seem to pluck out of some file and print over and over again. Three such stories, in particular, are so familiar that they virtually beg for new endings, which I will attempt to supply below.

* * * * * * * *

Retired senior citizen Frank "Hook" Dunker enjoys nothing better than fishing from the local pier. His enjoyment was recently shattered, however, when the band on his wristwatch snapped. He stared in dismay as his expensive timepiece bounced off the railing and fluttered out of sight in the murky green water below. Dunker figured he would never see his beloved watch again.

Exactly one week later, to the minute, Dunker was fishing from the exact same spot on the pier when he had a strike and pulled in an exceptionally large gafftopsail catfish. As he was about to throw it back, a friend stopped him by saying, "Hey! Those things are pretty good to eat. Why not try it?"

Already skimping on his food budget in order to save for a new watch, Dunker reluctantly agreed to take the catfish home.

That evening Dunker excitedly called his friend.

"I cleaned that catfish," he exclaimed, "and I can never thank you enough for convincing me to keep it.

"It was delicious."

* * * * * * * *

Angling enthusiast A. Savage Stryke, who moved to Florida several years ago and now lives within a few minutes' drive of two rivers, three lakes, eight canals, two bays and an inlet, was reminiscing recently about his early years in a small desert community.

"As a boy in New Mexico," Stryke said, "I used to read all the fishing books and magazines I could lay my hands on, but I never dreamed that one day I'd be living in a place where I could catch big fish every day of the week.

"Finally, last night, I dreamed it."

* * * * * * * *

Flyfisherman Walton Isaac Cray had been casting along a stream bank for nearly three hours. Despite his three-hundred- dollar custom graphite rod, weight-forward tapered line and impeccable custom flies, he had managed to catch only four 12-inch bass.

Rounding a bend, Cray came upon a barefoot lad wearing tattered overalls and a floppy straw hat. Clutched in the moppet's hand was a broom handle fitted with wrapping twine and a diaper pin. Baiting the giant safety pin with a chicken gizzard, the youngster tossed it into the water, then looked up at the flyrodder and flashed a disarming snaggletoothed grin from a cherubic mouth surrounded by a sea of freckles.

The angler's heart went out to this ill-equipped yet cheerful and determined tot.

"Here, son," he said, tendering a five-dollar bill. Take this money and go buy yourself a decent pole and a can of worms."

"Gee, thanks, mister," said the boy, his saucer eyes widening under an unruly mop of flame-red hair. Then, politely, he inquired of the flyfisherman, "You caught anything?"

"Only four small bass," Cray replied. "How about you?"

"Sure have," the waif exulted. "Lookit!"

He reached into a grimy burlap bag, previously unnoticed by the older angler, and withdrew from it two other five-dollar bills.

"You're the third sucker I caught today."

16

Son of Barge Canal

Except for an occasional reflexive spasm, the Cross-Florida Barge Canal is dead, but there are rumors that from its ashes will arise an even more gloriously ambitious undertaking—the North-South Barge Canal.

A premature leak from a suspect source indicates that the proposed North-South waterway will run from Miami straight up the middle of the peninsula, swerving to the Apalachicola River, then continuing via an out-of-state river network into the cotton belt and onward to America's heartland.

Aside from the sheer aesthetic value of such a waterway, planners foresee booming cross-commerce, built on southbound bales of cotton and northbound bales of marijuana.

Though still hush-hush in government circles, the canal project has so excited its proponents that a highly placed official in the Corps of Engineers, though begging to remain anonymous, could not contain himself from babbling on.

"We'll begin by re-routing the Apalachicola River," he said, drooling at the thought. "We'll build us a beauty of a dam near Blountstown and then take the river and cut us a sharp turn with that sucker over to around Lake City. From there—powee! A straight dragline shot south to Miami!"

Certain minor problems, he noted, can easily be licked, among them the re-location of Orlando.

17

"We'll move that whole place the heck out of the way, Mickey Mouse and all. Maybe park it in the Big Cypress or Gulf Hammock. All the picky little details haven't been worked out yet."

A significant fringe benefit will be the reclamation of Lake Okeechobee. Plans call for the lake to be drained and filled, thus turning useless water and weeds into hundreds of thousands of acres of valuable agricultural land. This will also eliminate the unsightly blotch made by Lake Okeechobee on color maps of Florida.

But all will not be converted to canefields. In keeping with the spirit of conservation historically linked to such projects, 75 acres of reclaimed land will be dedicated as the Okeechobee National Walking Catfish Refuge. Nor will recreational interests be ignored. The master plan includes a bingo hall near Belle Glade and a miniature golf course at Moore Haven.

"There's a lot of dirt to dig," the spokesman concluded, rubbing his hands, "but I can already envision the grand opening Barge-A-Cade tooting triumphantly through the middle of Florida, preceded by a vast school of grass carp chewing a path through the hyacinths and hydrilla, while thousands of proud Floridians line the banks in cheering throngs."

Although opposition to the canal is inconceivable, actual work will not begin until after the required public hearing, which is scheduled at 3:30 a.m. on Dec. 25 in the post office at Ochopee.

Additonal suggestions, if any, will be heard at that time.

Who Says This Is Fun?

Propagandists are out in the world spreading the rumor that fishing and hunting are fun and therefore immoral.

This really shouldn't disturb us too much because we have all been told since infancy that if you enjoy doing something it must be bad. Sex, for instance, should be practiced only with clinical detachment and for the sole and selfless purpose of procreation.

It doesn't surprise us, then, that the same indignant attitude is to be found among critics of the outdoor sports. There will always be those who claim that fun and sin are synonymous—like the spokeswoman for an anti-hunting group who was quoted in a Miami newspaper on National Fishing and Hunting Day as saying it is perfectly acceptable human behavior to practice consumerism on animals and animal products so long as you don't personally slay the beasts in the name of recreation.

In the same vein, Jacques Cousteau has passed judgment that it is ethically proper to catch fish for food—unless, of course, you have fun doing it. Then it's downright disgusting.

Neither critic, however, attempted to explain what difference it makes to the slain fauna, which would seem to be equally laid to rest in either case.

Outdoors publications make a poor podium from

which to hurl arguments at the many who assail fishing, hunting, guns and other outdoorsy things— for the obvious reason that their readers don't need any convincing, and those who do aren't famous for even acknowledging the existence of contradictory views, much less going in search of them in the pages of specialized magazines and books.

But by the same token, we can assume these words are pretty safe from the unapproving eyes of M'sieu Cousteau and his ilk: therefore, we can plot defensive strategy on behalf of the anti-fun movement.

Let's suppose a guardian of righteousness accuses you, in shocked tones, of fishing and/or hunting for the sheer enjoyment of the sport. You might answer: "You kidding? I only go because my wife runs me out from underfoot."

Or you might say you fish only reluctantly, to feed your cat. The moral complexities of this are so enormous that they will at least buy some peace while your spiritual advisor stops to ponder them. It would be inhumane, obviously, to deprive the cat of its favorite food. But should the cat's owner be allowed to catch that food himself? Or does morality dictate that the fish be caught only by commercial fishermen for conversion into Nine Lives?

Hunting is easily defended on grounds of fiscal duty. If you didn't hunt, who would pay the excise tax, buy duck stamps or purchase licenses and assorted permits. What fun is there in being bled dry?

You may run into a staunch reformist who refuses to accept any of these rebuttals. If so, arrange for him to meet you at the ramp after your next fishing trip. Let him watch you winch up the boat with blistered and bug-bitten arms. Open to his inspection your fish box, which contains two grunts, a squirrel fish, 10 dead shrimp, a soggy sandwich and an odor strong enough to dissolve a brick wall. Invite him to wash down the boat and pay to fill your gas tank.

Then ask him if he still thinks you do this for fun.

School's Out; New Names Needed

A recent *Florida Sportsman* article entitled "A Whisp of Snipe" elicited a correction from a self-styled "old snipe hunter" who said the correct term for a bunch of the tricky little shorebirds is "wisp" not "whisp." We had to search through three dictionaries before determining that he is right.

I personally think a more appropriate term would be "a snafu of snipe" but, anyway, this got me to thinking that the great majority of common furred and feathered animals are blessed with their own collective labels: for instance, a pack of wolves, a pride of lions, a skulk of foxes, a gang of elk, a covey of quail, a rafter of turkeys, a gaggle of geese. Some of those are familiar terms in everyday use. If you don't believe the others, you could look them up. They're real.

In many cases the group term has to do with some trait of the beasties being labeled. In a pride of lions, for example, old Leo not only has his pick of numerous lionesses, but then sits back and lets them bring home all of the bacon. Who couldn't take pride in an arrangement like that?

Yes, group names do help. Years ago when my elder son was seven, he already was an avid fisherman but not yet a hunter, even though he was familiar with all the common species of game that I bagged and brought home. One day while bank-fishing, he flushed his first covey of quail, whereupon he blurted out, "Wow! A whole school of quail!"

This little incident sharply illustrates the need for group names. Why is there a different collective label for just about every air-breathing species under the sun, but only one, "school," for all the fishes— from tuna weighing a thousand pounds to minnows weighing a thousand to the pound?

As any angler knows, the characteristics of various fish species are more than variable enough—and individual enough—to merit different group names. Try these:

A lurkage of largemouth bass, an inflation of blowfish, a mayhem of bluefish, an amputation of sharks, a prickle of pinfish, a subway of sardines, a measle of seatrout.

A rat-a-tat of drum, a belch of grunt, a steamroller of flounder, a puncture of catfish, a denture of barracuda, a cellblock of sheepshead, a harpoon of stingray.

And for the storied gamefish: a persnickety of permit, a snobbery of tarpon, a beeline of bonefish, a bedlam of bonito.

Some names, of course, could reflect current conditions: a mirage of kingfish, a fantasy of redfish.

I just hope we don't get into the labeling of people who are involved in fishing. If so, we might get: a fiction of outdoor writers.

Or even, I fear: an asylum of editors and a parsimony of publishers.

Protection from the Pelicans

At Flamingo in the Everglades National Park, which is one of the most popular launching spots for South Florida light-tackle anglers, the fish-cleaning table has lately been barricaded by an iron mesh enclosure so sturdy that it might lead visitors to believe some of the stories they hear about the size of Everglades mosquitoes (big enough to stand flat-footed and kiss a turkey).

On closer inspection, however, you discover that the barrier is twofold. An inconspicuous layer of standard fiberglass screen is actually what holds the skeeters at bay. The more noticeable iron grill was constructed to keep out winged pests of another sort—the loudest, largest, brashest and best organized band of thieving pelicans in the country.

There are two theories as to why the cleaning table, for years an open-air facility, was encased in iron. Spokesmen for the National Park Service, who should know, claim it was done to keep the fishermen from feeding the pelicans, even if most of the feeding was involuntary. After all, the policy of the current administration in Washington is to thin welfare ranks at all cost. Sloth and indolence are not to be tolerated, even among pelicans who, it is hoped, will now return to the Florida Bay work force and attempt to earn their own keep.

An alternate but unofficial explanation is that the pen was put up to protect the fishermen from the birds. This seems unlikely, considering that pelicans stand far higher on the Park's priority list than people do. But either way, anglers are grateful for the protection.

Those cleaning-table pelicans constituted more than a union. They were a guerrilla force, highly practiced, supremely determined and with a tactical flair worthy of Napoleon.

A lone fisherman at the table was lucky to get away with half his fish, for one man simply was no match for the insistent hordes of long-billed troops. The first platoon would advance frontally, but this was just a diversionary tactic so that the second and third platoons could effect a pincers movement around the flanks and make off with several fish before you noticed. And when finally you turned your attention to the perimeter, the main body would charge in and capture the only pompano you had caught in a year.

Occasionally one of the pelicans would add mayhem to larceny, although this was never done on purpose. One of them once aimed a typical awkward thrust at a trout I had just lifted from the cooler. I yanked the fish away, but there was no halting the momentum of the hooked bill, which flew like a blunted arrow to make a direct hit on the unsuspecting *derriere* of my fishing pal, who was turned toward the table, busily engaged in carving out some fillets.

Wounded only in the dignity, my companion's roar was one of outrage, not pain. He had always admired these beguiling birds, and talked baby talk to them, and fed them a fish carcass or two when he was sure the ranger wasn't around. Now he wore the kind of horrified, unbelieving look that might cross the face of a little girl who had been snapped at by Lassie.

After that moment of soul-searing betrayal, my friend never again spoke kindly of pelicans. Years later, in fact, he would respond to any mention of them by saying:

"Can't trust the damned things. Sneak up and bite you in the butt."

Yes, cleaning fish at Flamingo now is unbelievably uneventful. No longer is it necessary to simultaneously swat mosquitoes and parry the thrusts of hungry birds while you fillet your catch.

Luxury, sure. But there are those of us who miss the old days.

Test Your Angler Rating

In mulling over a suggestion that we run some sort of quiz every now and again, we did some research and discovered that quizzes are generally split into three categories: those that provide the reader with a psychological insight; those that provide the researcher with public trends and opinions; and those designed to show the reader that he doesn't know as much about the subject as the writer of the quiz does.

I discarded the last type immediately—not wishing to run the risk of having readers discover that they are smarter than I am. Finally, I hit on the idea of combining the first two types so that I would not have to think up two different quizzes. Now who's smart?

Score 10 points for every "A" response, five for every "B," three for every "C," two for every "D," and one for every "E."

1. What is your age?
   A. Under 39   B. 39   C. 39 and holding

2. How would you rate your angling skill?
   A. Superior   B. Outstanding   C. Excellent
3. What size fish do you catch most?
   A. Stupendous   B. Prodigious   C. Humongous
4. What kind of beverage do you prefer?
   A. Regular   B. Light   C. Imported
5. How often do you catch the limit?
   A. Regularly   B. Consistently   D. Continually
6. How often do you get skunked?
   A. Rarely   B. Infrequently   C. Seldom
7. What saltwater fish do you like most?
   A. Dolphin   B. Snook   C. Trout
   D. Kingfish   E. Redfish
8. What saltwater fish do you catch most?
   A. Crab   B. Catfish   C. Ray
   D. Needlefish   E. Blowfish
9. What freshwater fish do you like most?
   A. Largemouth bass   B. Striped bass
   C. Sunshine bass   D. Bream   E. Crappie
10. What freshwater fish do you catch most?
    A. Gar   B. Mudfish   C. Turtle
    D. Eel   E. Shiner
11. Do you ever combine fishing and camping?
    A. Yes   B. No
12. If yes, how often do you do it on purpose?
    A. Once in a while   B. Never

SCORING
  0-50: Terrible! Fish more!
  50-100: Not bad but you can do better! Fish more!
  100 and up: Too high! Quit thinking so much and fish more!

How to Tell If a Tale Is Tall

You've seen the light beer commercial where a lumberjack proclaims that he used to work in the "Sahara Forest"—implying that he did his job so marvelously well that the Sahara is now a desert. Not to be outdone, an angler in the same commercial describes how a giant bass pulled him up a waterfall.

Those are examples of what are popularly, but erroneously, known as tall tales. They aren't. These and similar stories foisted upon us as tall tales are really fairy tales—preposterous imaginings instantly recognizable as fantasy.

A real tall tale, while it has no more truth in it than a Hans Christian Andersen epic, must be a story that someone is *fully expected to believe*. Usually, but not always, that someone is a fisherman. Usually, probably always, he does believe.

That beer commercial contains a tall tale all right, but it has nothing to do with exterminated forests or fish that haul boats up waterfalls. The tall tale comes when both the lumberjack and the fishermen—already demonstrated liars—gaze innocently into the camera and tell us with a straight face that their watered-down brew "tastes great."

Great?

Pretty darn good, sure. Especially at high noon on a glassy sea. But *great*?

Anyway, the commercial demonstrates that a real tall tale, being one that the listener is expected to swallow, can be effectively aimed at beer drinkers, who will swallow anything with foam on the top. Still, the champion of all swallowers are fishermen. When it comes to tall tales, fishermen simply have no challengers, either as fabricators of them or suckers for them.

As a classic example, Angler A brings in a limit of bass, which he caught on live shiners just below the boat ramp. In answer to the eager questions of Angler B (his best friend since childhood), he describes how he caught them at four in the morning, eight miles up the river, in the middle of Turbid Slough, on a triple-bladed chartreuse spinnerbait with pink skirt.

Not only is Angler B humbly grateful for such generous information, but he is also amazed. Who else but his old buddy Angler A would even *think* to try a cast in Turbid Slough, considering that it is so shallow, muddy and smelly that even the gars and mudfish apparently shun it?

It turns out that Angler B is, for some inexplicable reason, unable to get a nibble in Turbid Slough, even after arriving at 3:30 a.m. and after having spent the entire previous afternoon searching tackle shops for the magic spinnerbait. But this is not what he tells Angler A.

He tells Angler A: "Thanks for the advice, pal. I did everything just like you said and I caught a limit weighing 64 pounds, 11 ounces."

"In Turbid Slough?" gasps Angler A.

"Of course, in Turbid Slough."

"At 4 in the morning?"

"Thereabouts."

"Say, buddy," says Angler A, "would you happen to have a spare triple-bladed chartreuse spinnerbait with a pink skirt? And could you lend me your alarm clock?"

Terror on Lake Talquin

I have been toying lately with the idea of going bream fishing after dark once more.

Toying, I said.

The tremors are not quite gone from my last night bream trip, which took place more than 25 years ago with my wife Cheryl and my son Dan, who was then seven or eight. The scene was Lake Talquin near Tallahassee, a reservoir rimmed by high and heavily wooded shores and bluffs.

As soon as I stopped the little wooden boat, Danny began to fidget. He was an avid fisherman, but now he eyed the impenetrable blackness of the forested bank before us with great trepidation, and suggested that we would probably catch more fish out in the middle of the lake. Motion denied.

Cheryl quickly pulled in a fat bream. She was delighted and Danny was at least momentarily motivated, although his sudden enthusiasm was just as suddenly quenched by the loud belch of a bullfrog.

"What was that?" Danny squealed.

"A frog," I told him.

"I doubt it," he said.

Cheryl yanked another bream from the water. "I got one," she announced. "Where did it go?"

The bewildered bluegill was swinging back and forth on the end of her line somewhere in space. We waved our arms around in its estimated path, recalculated the orbit and finally tracked it down.

Danny was hearing ever more threatening noises from shore. His urgent whispers of "What was that? What was THAT?" became a sort of cadence that I used to time my paddle strokes. Cheryl caught a lot of fish and was having a fine time. Danny caught some, but not enough to calm his suspicions as to what sort of unholy things were lurking in the night woods.

Suddenly, some sort of critter began violently shaking an overhead branch not 15 feet away from us. I thought perhaps it was a coon or possum fleeing up a tree limb from our approach. Danny thought perhaps it was the Creature from the Black Lagoon attempting to return to his watery home, only to find his path blocked by a flimsy boat containing two and a half bream fishermen.

At that moment, Cheryl had a bite and lifted her pole. The biggest bream of the night began flouncing loudly on the surface, echoing the noise from the bank and increasing the apprehension of the crew.

With extra effort, Cheryl finally pulled her big one

clear of the water. As usual, it sailed away into the wild black yonder, but this time it pendulumed straight back to deliver Cheryl a cold and scaly whack right in the neck. She naturally assumed that she was being attacked by flying alligators.

Cheryl's involuntary scream instantly ignited an even louder and longer one from Danny, who figured his only line of protection was crumbling.

Somehow, I managed to keep the boat from turning over. Somehow, I managed to get the outboard motor started with Danny clinging to the top of my head. Somehow, I found my way back to the landing.

Somehow, I don't think I'm quite ready for another night bream trip after all.

Lessons in Outdoor Writing

It is my distinct impression after these many years as an editor that half the boys in America think they would like to become outdoor writers, and half the men think that's what they are.

The boys send letters asking advice on pursuing such a career; the men send rambling accounts of their fishing and hunting adventures, and later send enraged protests upon having their creations rejected.

For some reason, there is so much interest in my humble trade that I have decided to devote this whole column to tips and instructions. Those few readers who have no interest in being an outdoor writer are excused.

A good way to get started is to write "how-to" stories. Here are a few suggested topics, applicable to various parts of the land:

"How to Build a Vacation Cabin out of Buffalo Chips."

"How to Use Camouflage for Sneaking out of the House."

"How to Call a Bull Moose by Bellowing a Promise You Don't Dare Keep."

"How to Appear Sane While Ice Fishing."

If you intend to specialize in hunting stories, take note that all hunters are preoccupied with animals' tails—possibly because they seldom glimpse any other part of the quarry's anatomy. At any rate, many game species are named, or nicknamed, for the color or shape of their tails.

For instance, you yourself may not know that those white things you occasionally see bobbing up and down in the myrtle bushes about a mile ahead of you are deer tails. Learning to recognize those and assorted other tails opens the door to not one but many article possibilities, starting with: "Whitetail— the Hunter's Favorite."

Once that story is on paper, you need only to switch all the "whites" in it to "black" and you have a new story about western hunting: "Blacktail—The Hunter's Favorite."

You're just getting started.

Go through the article and scratch out "big game" every time it appears and write in "small game." Erase ".243" and replace it with ".22." Now all that's left is to type the new title: "Cottontail—the Hunter's Favorite."

Replace ".22" with "shotgun" and mix in a sack of decoys. This gives you: "Pintail—The Hunter's Favorite."

Bring the .22 back and whistle up a pack of hounds. Now you have: "Ringtail—the Hunter's Favorite."

As you begin to explore ultimate truths, you will no doubt come up with a story entitled: "Tall tale—The Hunter's Favorite."

Later, without spoiling the continuity, you can even draw a word portrait of the nimrod himself: "Dragtail—The Hunter."

And eventually you will spend enough time in camp to emerge with the definitive piece of the entire series:

"Cocktail—The Hunter's *Real* Favorite."

Advertising Copy Made Easy

My recent column of lessons on outdoor writing did not garner the acclaim I anticipated. To the contrary, a number of readers wrote to express indignation that I had wasted their time by expounding on a trade that is suited only to the eternally immature.

Those readers insisted on receiving instruction in some field of writing which, while equally unfettered by fact, is more likely than outdoor writing to someday fulfill the American dream of three-piece suits and three-martini luncheons.

The one discipline that meets those requirements is, of course, the writing of advertising and/or public relations copy. Fortunately, I know this subject well enough to give lessons, although too well to take it up myself.

If you're serious about this, a good way to begin your long climb toward the snow-covered heights of the advertising game is to use the "confidence building" angle in your early work. A textbook example is the slogan that you see in so many lure ads: "Made BY Fishermen FOR Fishermen."

Now that is powerful ad writing. It gives the angler a heap of confidence to know that he will not be fishing with something that was made BY bowlers FOR golfers. The one problem with this angle has to do with repeat sales, inasmuch as the carefully instilled confidence generally lasts only until the buyer gets a chance to fish the lure. After a couple of hours without a strike he suddenly begins to suspect that his new gadget might have been made BY hopscotchers FOR ropejumpers, and by the end of the fishless day he is firmly convinced it was made either BY Democrats FOR Republicans or BY tenants FOR landlords.

You needn't worry much about repeat sales, however, as the rise of the average copywriter is so meteoric that you will probably be with your third or fourth agency by the time that lure ad comes out. If you are still in Florida, you probably will be working for a real estate developer and busy thinking up exotic names for various mutilated portions of the landscape.

These eyesores should wear titles such as Beercan Bay, Dragline Lagoon, Landfill Acres, Outfall Isles, Pesticide Point, Hydrilla Haven, Erosion Beach, Scratchbite Shores, Ditchside Heights, Cowchip Ranches and Eutrophic Lakes.

As an ambitious copywriter, however, you learn to use your keyboard like a magic wand, and with a few clacks transform those developmental monstrosities into: Shangri-La, Champagne Shores, Idyllic Acres, Ponderosa Plains, Redwood Ravines, Heavenly Hills, Valhalla Vale, Polynesian Paradise, Crystal Waters and the Glades of Euphoria.

If there are no ponderosas or redwoods in Florida, and precious few lumps that might pass as hills, so much the better for your copywriting reputation. You will probably get a bonus.

Another can't-miss ad trick is to convince the consumer that he deserves something bigger than he can handle, or more expensive than he can afford, in order to maintain his image. I saw a recent example of this in promotional copy about a cavernous new 172-quart fisherman's ice chest, the biggest made. The copy proclaims that this cooler "holds a full day's catch."

Not for me, it doesn't. I'll take two.

You Too Can Write a Show

Past columns have provided valuable educational guidance for those interested in careers as outdoor writers and advertising copywriters. One closely allied field, the scripting of television fishing shows, remains to be covered. In sheer job opportunity this must be the richest field of all, judging from the vast number of such shows that stalk the cable at ridiculous hours.

The work is tricky because it requires a mix of both advertising and outdoor writing skills, but if you are an aspiring piscatorial playwright be not dismayed. Only the most meager sprinkling of those talents is needed, and your mental burden will be further mitigated by the fact that once you finish writing your first script you will never have to create another. The minor changes called for from week to week can be accomplished with a small eraser and a short pencil.

Although many fishing shows are on the air, their scripts are indistinguishable. You can check this for yourself by quickly spinning the channel knob on your cable-fitted TV set. You will note a fishing program on every other channel and, as you flick the dial, you will be able to follow a single strain of dialogue without interruption, even though different

37

shows and different voices click on and off. You will hear something like this:

Channel R: *"That's a real . . ."*
Channel T: *". . . purty fish, good buddy."*
Channel V: *"Yeah, good buddy . . . ."*
Channel X: *"That's a real . . ."*
Channel Z: *". . . purty fish."*

I should have mentioned earlier that a simple test is available to determine one's psychological proclivity for this line of work. The applicant is shown a sizable largemouth bass—belly distended, jaws agape, eyes bulging—and if he blurts out, "Yuck. Ugly!" he fails the aptitude test. All television catches are "purty fish."

Of course, as a writer you will have to change the guest introduction each week, but you will need only three basic intros—one for country-western singers, one for aging athletes and one for world-class scientists. An example of the latter follows:

Host: Our guest is my ol' buddy Dr. Billy Joe Daggett, the famous bio-capitalist and dean of the Ichthyological Merchandising Department at Southern State College. I guess we can thank ol' Dr. Billy Joe for about half the bass we catch any more, what with the amazing scientific discoveries he keeps pulling out of his lab. His newest is the Daggett Dynaphotosmellometer, which is a combination light-level sensor, pH meter and sound emitter that lays out an irresistible trail of fish-attracting . . .

You get the idea. With the appearance of each new guest scientist, you have to change only the good doctor's name and the name of his best-selling gadget. It is a good idea to associate him with a college, even if he only lives near one.

Similarly if the new guest is a country-western singer, you drop in the name of the person and the name of the album, and if the guest is a former athlete, you verify the spelling of his name, then mention the game he used to play and the last year in which he was allowed to play it.

And *never* mention the name Lucy Ricardo. That's the show after yours.

Now, Meet the Croonbait

As one might imagine, the annual introduction of new and "different" fishing lures is a mammoth headache for the tackle industry. Like automobiles, lures have long since run the gamut of available designs and now must rely for annual sales punch on cosmetics.

In a less complicated era, baits were painted such mundane colors as green, to suggest a frog; blue, to suggest a mullet; pearl, to suggest a shad. Artistic touches were pretty much limited to globular eyes and screened scalation.

Fish seemed to like the old look pretty well. But fish do not buy lures.

As the sport and industry burgeoned, the problem

of attracting buyer attention away from dozens of competitors grew complex indeed. Eventually, manufacturers could not deal in mere "colors" at all, but were forced to produce lures of such lifelike finish, such variety and subtlety of hue and shade, such faithful imitation of actual species, that the angler had to take care not to fry them when hastily cooking up a mess of panfish.

And now the possibilities in lifelike baits seem exhausted. There are replicas of bass and bluegill, crappie and chub, striper and sunfish, ballyhoo and bonito, dolphin and dace, pinfish and pumpkinseed—in short, just about every species yet identified in lake or sea.

One manufacturer, casting frantically about for any species at all which has not yet been immortalized in a blister pack, is said to have found that the only two fish left unimitated by luremakers are the coelacanth and the whale shark, neither of which he judged to have much commercial appeal.

As a result of this dead end, he hit upon the brilliant idea of abandoning altogether the quest for a new look, and to develop instead new sounds. Since sound-producing lures are presently in the same embryonic stage as colors were in long years past—that is, they make only the most basic of noises, such as rattles, glubs, blurps, buzzes and hums—it seemed logical to him that the company which first introduced new concepts of polytonality would be bound to prosper.

He assembled a team of engineers and musicians and charged them with developing a lure which he plans to call the Croonbait. Our Industrial Espionage Subscription Service (IESS) reports that it looks something like an ocarina with treble hooks. It has a series of small apertures along the lateral line, and an internal system of reed valves which regulate a flow of water at programmed intervals.

Anglers are known to dote on "tuned" baits, and each Croonbait will be factory pre-tuned—with *real* tunes, all of them authorized by the composers' guild.

Various regional models will be marketed: the "Yankee Doodle Dandy" for the North; the "Redneck National Anthem" for the South; "California, Here I Come" for the Pacific Coast; "La Cucaracha" for Mexican bass lakes.

The biggest seller of all is projected to be a special combination saltwater-freshwater model: "Porgy and Bass."

The Collections— Hers and Mine

One of the world's most extensive collections of strange and ancient foodstuffs belongs to my wife, who has compiled it over many years by bringing home doggie bags from restaurants in various states and hemispheres and storing them in our refrigerator. I have no doubt that this collection will continue to grow during our remaining days on earth and, when willed to the Smithsonian or other worthy institution, will afford life's work for a team of research scientists that will attempt to identify and catalog it.

Good luck to them. By comparison, sorting out the species involved in the evolution of man is an undergraduate exercise.

Not that the relationship of everything in the collection to known substances is indeterminable. Poking through individual containers with a fork, you occasionally hear the unmistakable "ping" of an agatized pea or the more solid "clunk" of a petrified potato. But only a ranking paleontologist would even dare guess at the origins of what appear to be the fossilized remains of dozens of assorted fowl, sea creatures and ruminant mammals.

In its entire history, as I recall, only one item has ever been lost from the collection, and that by accident. While the bags were being routinely dusted and restacked, one fell to the floor and burst, whereupon the contents were gulped down by the dog, who immediately fell into a drooling swoon—not because of ancient toxins in the one-time foodstuffs but simply from the shock of finally getting to eat something from a doggie bag.

Of course, my wife denies that it is a collection at all. She says the stuff is in there because some day we are going to eat it. Boy, do I hope she is wrong!

She obviously is wrong when she attempts to liken her compulsion for doggie bags to my own constrained compiling of outdoor sports equipment—equipment that will surely prove useful in the future, and possibly even necessary. Oh, she long ago accepted my assurance that I need a different rod and reel for every species of fish, and a different size and color of lure, too. But she questions why I need three rifles in order to take one shot at a deer every four or five years.

Patience, I tell myself. Surely she knows that I will have to acquire even more rifles down the line if I am to be prepared for woods hunting, plains hunting, mountain hunting, jungle hunting and all the other kinds of hunting that occasionally flicker through my fantasies. No need to mention that I generally use my old shotgun for that one shot I get at a deer every few years.

She also wonders why I own so many knives, and how they manage to reproduce so prolifically. No mystery there. A deer must be bled, gutted, skinned, halved, quartered, butchered and sliced, using a different blade for each purpose. And that says nothing of the knives needed for small game, fish and survival. Check any mail order catalog if you doubt me.

Though they seem nothing alike, my wife's collection and mine really have a symbiotic relationship. Every time I get a new piece of equipment, she gets a new doggie bag. From one of the best restaurants in town.

Almost, But Not Quite

If you've watched all those movies about the lives of famous inventors, you can be excused for thinking that great ideas invariably come as isolated thunderbolts of inspiration. The fact is, that for every invention that clicks there are probably dozens of similar ones that narrowly miss making the grade because of minor conceptual flaws.

Consider, for instance, an angler who first hammered a kitchen spoon until it became a fishing lure, and then fitted it with a tail he carved from a chunk of bacon rind. Coincidentally, and at about the same time, another fisherman was also designing a lure made from kitchen components, but he selected a fork and fitted it with a strip of leftover macaroni.

As we all know by now, the spoon-and-rind has survived the test of time, but the fork and macaroni somehow failed to catch the public fancy—or that of the fish, which probably could not forgive the omission of the cheese sauce.

History records other instances when nearly identical concepts met vastly different fates at public hands. Everybody knows about the Book-of-the-Month Club, a great and continuing financial success. But few are aware that the Cat-of-the-Month Club was conceived a short time later and with the same set of inducements—five free cats upon joining, and then the opportunity to keep or send back a different breed of cat each month at rock-bottom price. The club folded after selling only one membership, that to a woman who bought it as a gift for her husband's ex-wife.

A current enterprise may be destined for the same fate. A company is advertising "aroma discs," which are played much like musical records but which emit scents instead of sounds. Good idea? Sure. But the selection of scents offered may prove to be the project's downfall. The stated aim is to "bring forth your most exhilarating memories," but the aromas listed, though pleasant enough, are common ones that most of us have sniffed far too often to associate with specific memories.

If you would conjure up nostalgia it must be done with nearly unique smells—smells that smash instantly through the barriers of time and project images as vivid as those on a movie screen.

For fishermen, the necessary assortment of smells would be a snap. A disc dispensing the pungent aroma of rotten eggs, though gagging all others present, would instantly focus a snook fisherman's mind on low tide in the mangroves—and the time he caught a limit of 20-pounders from a deep hole in the middle of the aromatic mudflats.

45

Want to bring back the headboat trip when you caught all those flag yellowtail and big snapper? Two scents played simultaneously—ground chum and diesel fumes—should do it. And for the hunter, a disc entitled "feather pillow on fire" is sure to bring back the mouth-watering aroma of last year's camp-roasted duck.

I could think up more scents for the sportsman's library of treasured odors, but I have to go now. Cooking is my hobby and I have this idea for a new dessert that I'm going to call pineapple rightside-up cake.

My All-Time Top Ten Alibis

Lists of 10 are stylish these days, so to stay in style I present my list of 10 all-time fishing and hunting alibis. You may decide whether they are the 10 best or 10 worst. I only say they are my 10 favorites, and that I actually heard every one of them. Cross my heart!

1. The fishing camp manager said bream were so thick and ravenous that it would be no trick at all to catch a limit on flies, so the eager customer rented a boat and motor, picked up his flyrod, and sallied forth. I was present hours later when he returned, breamless and boiling. "No wonder you didn't catch any," said the manager, pointing to the popping bug on the angler's leader. "I told you to use a white bug with black dots. That's a black bug with white dots."

2. I watched at the ramp as a lone boater began woefully winching in the sunken skiff he had launched without its plug. While he cranked, he grumbled. "It's my wife's fault. I *told* her to make sure the plug is in before she lets me drive away from the house."

3. The end of his monofilament line showed definite proof that a poor knot had been the reason for my companion's lost fish. As diplomatically as possible, I offered to show him a stronger knot. "I can tie good knots," he responded in a huff. "I just don't do it because when a fish breaks off above the knot you lose too much line."

4. This one I've heard at least 30 times in 30 years—always after a good fish has been lost at boatside. "I quit bringing the landing net because I just don't need it that often."

5. In a tackle store I listened to a sad stranger explain why he had caught no bass the day before,

even though others on the same lake had reported fine action. "The bass were hitting six-inch worms, but all I had with me were nine-inchers."

6. Stuck on a Florida Bay mud flat for hours, the weekend skipper was furious. "The chart for this area is no good," he fumed. "It tells you where things are but it doesn't tell you you can't get to them."

7. Two of three hunters in a blind had killed teal when a small flock flew over. The third claimed he had scored too, yet no dead duck could be seen on his side of the boat, even though the water was open and teal are not divers. Pressed by his gloating buddies to point out his duck or admit that he was the only one who missed, he said: "This gun has an extra-full choke. I put so many shot into him that he sank."

8. A veteran trapshooter, after missing his first shot and then running 24 straight, alibied his miss by pointing out that he had accidentally left an empty shell in the off-barrel of his over-under, and that this had destroyed the gun's balance on that first shot.

9. Returning empty-handed to dock, a Gulf Coast fisherman explained why he had lured no trout to his plugs. "The water is too hot. It makes the trouts' mouths so tender that they won't hit hard lures."

10. A deer hunter staggered into camp after dark, much to the relief of his campmates who had been looking for him nearly all afternoon. "I wasn't bad lost," claimed the prodigal. "I just ran across one of the dogs and figured he knew a quicker way back to camp. Turned out the damn dog was lostern' I was."

From Rabbits to Riches

The solution to this country's unemployment problem is as near as the corner newsstand, where the ads in a single copy of a famous outdoor magazine offer literally dozens of career opportunities—more than enough to put to work every pair of idle hands in the Far West, Midwest, Deep South and parts of the Shallow South.

You can, for instance, earn fabulous sums by operating a mail-order business (right from your own home!) or, if you have a callused thumb and hyperactive salivary glands, by stuffing and sealing envelopes.

Should you care for a more romantic job, there's an ad in which a rugged individual wearing a 1918 army campaign hat challenges you to "Train for an Outdoor Job as a Ranger or Game Warden." And if wearing antique hats is not your dream, you could "Be Your Own Boss as a Chimney Sweep." Naturally, you would be your own boss. Who else would let a chimney sweep boss him around? Some of the jobs described in the magazine offer nothing more than lifetime security, but many promise riches untold. And if your cherished hope is to someday head a giant conglomerate, why you can clip a few coupons and do that too. Here's how: First you answer the ad that says, "Earn Amazing Profits. Raise Rabbits." A nondreamer would be content to raise his rabbits and sell them for the amazing profits. But thou, as a budding

tycoon, see this particular enterprise as a building block for all kinds of wheeling and dealing.

You answer another ad and find out how to
"Make and Sell Traps and Cages." You make
traps and cages. Then thou start turning loose
rabbits. Soon, every soul in the neighborhood runs
to your door, frantically waving dollar bills and
screaming for traps and cages. Your rabbits cooper-
ate only too gladly in this venture and as their pro-
duction soars, new cage and trap customers pour in
from other neighborhoods, and then from surround-
ing counties.

Eventually, traps and cages alone cannot stem the
flood of rabbits. But thanks to another of those ads,
you are ready. You "Learn Gun Repair." Every rusty
gun in town is hauled out of its closet and rushed to
you for overhaul so it can be pressed into service
against the rabbits. Your "Amazing Profits" already
have tripled, but more will come.

So enthusiastic are your brood rabbits about this
business that no amount of traps, cages and newly
repaired guns can keep up with their pace, so finally
the entire population of the city runs inside and calls
you up, because you have long since answered yet
another ad and learned to "Be a Locksmith." Now
you take orders for repair work on existing locks and
for new rabbit-proof installations.

Has the rabbit business run its course at last? Not
for a minute. You own an inexhaustible supply of
rabbits. And you have answered an ad that vows to
teach you how to "Mount Birds, Fish and Animals."

Rabbits' feet, anyone?

A Word We've
Always Needed

"Frammer."

You won't find the word in Webster's because it was invented in their teen-age years by my son Dan and his hunting-fishing buddy Jim Kaple. So valuable is this word, however, that I may write a dictionary myself just so it can be officially recorded.

This is its definition: *Frammer: "A hopelessly inept hunter, fisherman or camper; an outdoorsman who should never have walked out the door."*

Mind you, it doesn't mean a novice. We are all novices at the start. We make our mistakes and we learn from them and we advance in our outdoor education. A frammer never learns because he never truly grasps what is going on out there.

There have been frammers throughout history, of course, although in past times the word was not available to label them as such. One whom I remember vividly from my reading was a 1930s explorer who lugged an outboard motor all the way across the Andes to the headwaters of the Amazon, not realizing until he arrived weeks later that outboard motors thrive only when fed a constant diet of gasoline—a commodity not likely to be encountered for the first few thousand miles of the journey downriver.

51

Later, while still thousands of miles from anywhere, the same fellow spotted a small snake in the bottom of his dugout canoe, and chose to defend himself with a shotgun instead of a stick. The snake went to the bottom of the river, but so did the canoe and numerous items of irreplaceable equipment.

The first frammers to bear the name were encountered by Dan and Jim one November day about a mile north of the Tamiami Trail in the Everglades. There were three of them and they were engaged in kicking and cursing an ancient and recalcitrant swamp buggy which, judging from what dibbles and dabs of conversation the boys were able to pick up, had been purchased only the week before at a towering price. Yet on this its maiden voyage under new ownership, it had taken fully two hours to lumber a mile from the main road.

Finally the old machine coughed and expired there in the marsh, like a dying elephant that had courageously managed to stagger against all odds to its legendary burial ground. From the agonized noises it had made toward the last, Dan and Jim figured the transmission had shed all its teeth.

The three owners circled their dead vehicle, held brief council and then decided on a course of treatment.

They installed a new oil filter.

When this failed to revive the mechanical beast, they shouldered their new shotguns and began plodding dejectedly toward the highway.

Afterward, as Dan and Jim sat resting, their eyes fell upon the discarded box whence came the oil filter that had so miserably failed to cure the swamp buggy. On the box was printed the brand name "Fram."

The boys began to giggle. No offense, Fram, but the perfect word literally jumped forth.

"Frammer" was born, and a serious gap in the English language was at last filled.

New Horizons for Angling Snobbery

Many years ago, having fallen under the evil influence of zealous competitive fishermen, I temporarily took leave of my senses and became a practicing purist.

I blush to recall it now, but I shuddered at the thought of using natural bait in any form for any kind of angling. I even considered trolling as a blot upon one's character. The only acceptable way of fishing was to cast artificial lures. But, being open-minded, my co-purists and I at least condoned three kinds of lure-tossing tackle—spinning, plugcasting and fly.

I was brought back to earth one day by a sharp exchange of words between my two sons, then seven and five. Dan, the elder, was crowing about some mackerel he had caught. David indignantly pointed out that he had caught some too.

"Yeah," Danny said, his voice fairly dripping with scorn and derision, "but you got yours on *bait.*"

This demonstrates that the pestilence of snobbery may strike at any age. I am happy to report that both Dan and I recovered fully. He now does most of his fishing with live shrimp, and if I still lean heavily upon lures, it's mostly because I want to avoid the headaches of catching and/or keeping live bait. Dabs of dead bait are often to be found on my jigs.

I only bring it up because the art of angling snobbery has lately taken a most surprising turn. It used to be a simple enough thing to follow: the dry-fly fisherman looked down his nose at the wet-fly fisherman, who looked down his nose at the bass-bugger, who looked down his nose at the topwater plug fisherman, who looked down his nose at the crankbaiter, who looked down his nose at the flinger of plastic worms.

All, of course, looked down their collective noses at users of natural bait, live or dead. Where is the challenge, they asked, in convincing a fish that he should feed on his natural prey?

Whether or not you agreed with any of it, there was no mystery involved. A purist was someone who stuck to his artificial lures come shoal or high water.

Now, however, the ancient order of things is under blatant attack by a group of offshore fishermen who have banded together and issued the pronouncement that it is unsportsmanlike to catch billfish by trolling with artificial lures. Their approved way is to drag dead, rigged, natural baits.

Such an ethical involution of the traditional code of purism may require years to fathom, even with the efforts of our finest philosophers—especially since those same anglers agree that *live bait* is just as reprehensible as artificial lures. Nothing but dead fish will do. Perhaps, by special dispensation, they might allow a dead squid.

Only once before have I ever heard anyone attack the propriety of artificial lures, and that objection was made on humane grounds, having nothing to do with sportsmanship.

Ernie Lyons, for years a much-admired columnist in the Stuart *News*, said it was unkind enough to catch a fish by offering him a free meal; to deny him even that last pleasure was downright immoral.

That was Ernie's way of defending his own pet angling approach. I think. Anyway, it would be tough for Ernie or anyone else to define a purist these days.

If You Bag It, Eat It

One of the few verses I ever committed to memory hung on the wall of a Central Florida hunting lodge:

> *Game is plover, quail, partridge, grouse.*
> *So is elephant—and sometimes mouse.*

This is more than just a pleasant little rhyme. It hints at a most serious problem that any hunter—or fisherman—might suddenly have to face.

The hunter, let's say, nestles his trusty 20-gauge in the crook of his arm and sallies forth after partridge —only to have his faithful spaniel flush, instead, an elephant. Even as he fires and hollers, "Fetch," the nimrod begins to comprehend the problem.

In the same vein, let's say that a fisherman grabs his spinning rod and sets out after a mess of grunts to fry for his supper, but all at once finds himself hooked up to a blue marlin. While reaching for the landing net, he too must begin puzzling over the problem.

By now, devoted readers of this column will have divined the question that so perplexes our two intrepid outdoorsmen:

"How in the world do you cook this thing?"

The angler never having done anything in the kitchen except fry up a mess of bream, snapper or grunts, would obviously have to dope out his own approach to cooking a blue marlin. It would go something like this:

FRIED MARLIN AND HUSH PUPPIES

1 marlin	10 pounds flour
25 pounds corn meal	1 pound black pepper
5 pounds salt	100 gallons vegetable oil

Heat oil to 375 degrees in a cast-iron bathtub. Skin and draw marlin, removing head and bill. With a chainsaw, score marlin several times on each side. Mix corn meal, flour and salt in the bottom of a canoe. Add the marlin and dredge thoroughly. Drop into hot oil and fry two hours on each side, turning once. Remove with a forklift and drain on double roll of newsprint. Serve piping hot with a six-foot mound of two-pound hushpuppies. Serves five (neighborhoods).

Similar improvisation would be required of that lucky hunter who bagged the elephant. His culinary experience being limited to the roasting of game birds, that influence surely would be felt as he set about to create his elephant recipe:

ROAST STUFFED ELEPHANT

1 elephant, scraped and drawn (reserve giblets)
1/4 acre onions, 1/2 acre celery
6004 loaves stale bread
398 loaves stale cornbread
100 pounds butter, softened
50 pounds seasoned salt
1 orchard of sage
1 anchovy (if desired)

Boil elephant giblets for three days. Remove from broth and chop fine. Chop onions and celery. Toss all ingredients into a cement mixer and mix well. Add giblet broth sparingly, a few gallons at a time, until dressing reaches desired consistency. Stuff elephant and secure opening with skewers (blue marlin bills make fine elephant skewers). Bake two weeks in an abandoned municipal incinerator with heat on medium-low. Turn out on a bed of palm fronds and place a watermelon in the elephant's mouth. Serves everybody.

Elephant Cuisine
Goes International

What to do about all these elephant recipes? That is the question.

Since printing my instructions for roasting an elephant, I have been deluged by mail from readers, all of them offering additional recipes. Space being limited, I am compelled to choose only one for this column.

But how to decide which is best? I couldn't stand the thought of trying them all, or even a single one, because we still have 981 doggie bags in our refrigerator that my wife brought home after the big elephant roast last January. (Yes, we tried getting a dog. No, the dog wouldn't eat the leftover elephant. Yes, we got rid of the dog. No, we didn't get rid of the doggie bags.)

Finally I decided just to use the recipe that had found its way to my desk from the longest distance. It comes from George E. Davy, of Uplands, Blatchington Hill, Seaford, Sussex, England. If that's not an old elephant hunter's home address, I'll eat my hunting books.

"As this is open season for elephant recipes," Mr. Davy wrote, "I enclose my contribution, which I hope you will enjoy. This recipe was given to me on a recent visit to Victoria Falls, Zimbabwe, and I'm sure you'll agree it's quite appetizing. Keep up the good work. I do enjoy my *Florida Sportsman*.

Even considering Mr. Davy's flattery and everything, I still hesitated before printing his recipe. That's because it comes from Africa, where elephants in most areas, being seriously threatened by poachers, are protected by law.

But things are different here in Florida, where there is no closed season on elephants, nor even a bag limit, so I don't suppose it will do any harm to use another elephant recipe. If it were a redfish recipe, forget it.

ELEPHANT STEW

1 medium size elephant (Loxodontus africana)
20 bags salt, 500 kg peppercorns
750 bushels potatoes, 125 bushels carrots
2000 sprigs parsley, 1 rabbit

"Cut elephant into bite-size chunks; this will take about six weeks. Chop vegetables into cubes (another four weeks). Place meat in jumbo-size missionary pot. Pump in 5000½ litres of elephant gravy and simmer for 28 days. Shovel in salt and pepper.

"When meat is tender add vegetables. To speed up matters it is recommended that the vegetables be added with a steam shovel. Simmer slowly for another week, then garnish with parsley. Serves approximately 3000 people.

"If additional guests are expected, add the rabbit. However, this is not really recommended because very few people like hare in their stew."

And Now, the Envelope, Please

Did you know that the Roper Poll came up with a list of the 10 foods that most people consider most repulsive?

Probably you didn't. The results were not widely broadcast on television because the announcers threatened to strike if forced to read the list out loud. One dared to try, and was said to have erupted in living color halfway between No. 5 and No. 6.

But I will go ahead and print the list because readers of this column, being fishermen, are not easily dismayed by disgusting things. In fact, many of you will be personally familiar with some of these very substances, having used them for bait, chum or fertilizer.

Whether even a fisherman would venture to use any of them as food opens another debate. My guess is that everything on the list should be considered too good to put in a fisherman's lunch but too gross to put on his family table. Anyway, here is the list of "winners":

1. Snails.   2. Brains.   3. Squid.
4. Shark.   5. Tripe.   6. Kidneys.   7. Tongue.
8. Oxtail.   9. Squab.   10. Mussels.

To which I add my personal critique of each in turn:

Snails. With this I have to agree. I tried snails once and found them to be marginally edible after energetic pounding with a heavy hammer. Even then they were much too crispy to suit me, and much too similar in taste to something called *escargots* that once darkened my plate at a fancy restaurant.

Brains. Why wasn't this No. 1?

Squid. Snappers adore squid, and snappers are a lot fussier about their food than I am. But for my part, squid should be served at the rate of one pound per quart of ketchup.

Shark. This one is a maybe. Like possum, the quality of shark meat will depend upon what the critter has been eating lately. If Republican-fed, it would probably be tender and plump. Sharks on a diet of Democrats would be lean and stringy.

Tripe. This is a ringer. Tripe is something you read, not something you eat (no smart remarks, please).

Kidneys. My only experience eating kidney had to do with a dish called steak and kidney pie. They were kidding about the steak, but not, unfortunately, about the kidney.

Tongue. How anyone could bear to eat something that came out of an animal's mouth is beyond me. I'll stick to eggs, thank you.

Oxtail. This has to be a big improvement over tongue, but I'm still more of a middle-of-the-roader.

Squab. Let's get serious. The only people who would put squab on a list of worst foods are those who have smelled a pigeon's nest. Those who haven't will gladly pay $13.95 a pound for squab and are glad to get it.

Mussels. Thumbs down. These are as objectionably crunchy as snails and of a funereal color to boot.

All in all, I think I'll take peanut butter.

Son of Nausea

You'd think that the Roper Poll's list of disgusting foods would be enough to make anyone drop the magazine and rush from the living room with his hands over his mouth. But no. Readers are insisting that I disclose my own nominations.

My stomach may not be strong enough to get through 10 of them but I will name a few—not one of which is something I just made up. Each is a dish I have tried (or tried to try), or noticed on a label or menu, or read about, or seen on television. They are given in no special order, except for No. 1, which is the clear Grand Champion of Grossouts.

I'm referring to a carp dish that was featured, live, several years ago on a television show with

Walter Cronkite. It wasn't the show that was live; it was the carp.

Anyway, there was Walter Cronkite sitting in an elegantly decorated restaurant somewhere in China, obviously hoping against hope that they were about to serve him some chow mein or moo goo gai pan. Instead, his worst fears were surpassed when the waiter set before him an enameled plate on which reposed a big-eyed, pucker-mouthed, gasping, flopping carp, which had only just begun to apprehend that it was the intended entree.

As a crowning touch, some sort of rare and exotic sauce had been ladled over the protesting fish. The carp, in turn, was courteously passing most of this sauce along to Mr. Cronkite's necktie, by means of frantic sweeps of its muscular tail.

The ingredients of the sauce were never mentioned but we can easily guess one of them, contributed by the fish itself. As I recall, Mr. Cronkite did not finish his meal—or even start it. For that matter, this affair may have been what finally ended his television career. He was already in semi-retirement at the time, and I don't recall having seem him on the tube since.

While one would have to travel all the way to China to sample live carp with fertilizer sauce, that isn't quite far enough to make me feel completely at ease.

Running a close second in sheer repulsiveness to live carp is, of course, dead carp, freshly caught, cleaned and cooked.

Raw fish in general does not place very high on my

gustatory list, even when I do not have to kill it at the table. True, I have eaten some kinds of raw fish that were merely tasteless, but there are other kinds that could turn a pelican into a vegetarian.

As for canned foods, this category is a tie between "Brains in Natural Juices" and "Octopus in Its Own Ink," both of which I have seen on grocer's shelves. Happily, I can't remember where.

Although organ meats rank low on most lists, I admit to a liking for liver. However, I have steadfastly refused to sample prairie oysters (a product of the conversion of young bulls into steers) even though they are reputed to have a most distinctive, nut-like flavor.

From Rags to High Fashion

Most modern sportsmen are release-minded. They even use barbless hooks so that fish can be turned loose with little handling, if any at all. They do this because it helps preserve fish for the future. But even more, they do it to keep from getting fish slime on their designer clothes.

These days it's more difficult to stay in style than it is to tie knots, rig rigs or make sense of all the new fishing regulations. And particularly difficult for us older folks who remember simpler times when you wore your good clothes until they became stained, faded or wrinkled beyond all hope of ironing, at which time you re-assigned them to your fishing wardrobe.

Now, following the dictates of fashion, you have to go down to the department store and *buy* stained, faded and wrinkled clothing at outrageous prices —and not to fish in at all, or even to wear while changing the grease in your outboard motor, which is what you'd naturally think they were designed for. No you buy them to wear to school, to the office, to dinner, to concerts, to parties, to ballgames, to dances and to weddings.

Had we been able to foresee this fashion phenomenon some decades ago, my wife and I would have been able to stockpile enough designer clothes to fund a lavish retirement. Back then, the kids generally returned from fishing so encrusted that they could barely move. My wife's routine was first to hose them down enough to verify that they were her own, after which she commenced to scrape off layers with a putty knife until she reached either fabric or skin. If any of the former remained, she would pry it off and deposit it at arm's length in the washing machine. What came out looked exactly like what you now pay 95 dollars for in the boutiques.

It's strange indeed that fishing is the one activity for which ratty-looking clothes are no longer socially acceptable. Having been deprived of our traditional angling raiment, we would all be fishing in the nude by now if the mail order houses and sportsmen's shops had not charged in to fill the void with new lines of custom-designed, color-coordinated, hand-tailored fishing outfits. They are expensive, of course, costing almost as much as the disreputable rags that fill the fashion malls, but fishermen have to wear *something*.

There are pitfalls to beware of, though, in ordering from the catalogs. For instance, you could become the laughing stock of the bonefish flat by showing up in a shirt with a rainbow trout embroidered on the pocket or, more mortifying yet, a mallard duck.

And think of the ostracism that would greet an angler caught carelessly wearing a Keys guide cap in salmon country or a deerstalker on the tarpon grounds of Homosassa.

If in doubt, it's pretty safe to spend high. Orvis has a pair of boat mocs that cost $165. I have owned several *boats* that didn't cost $165, so I'm sure that no matter where you wore those mocs, your sartorial taste would never be questioned, not even if everyone else were wearing L.L. Bean Pacs or Gore-Tex walkers.

Things are even tougher for hunters, who must change their entire wardrobes every year, from parkas to underpants, just to stay abreast of the latest designs in camouflage.

New camouflage patterns are big business. Hoping to crash the action, I designed a new pattern myself the other day, but now I can't find it.

Time for Some New Advice

An adage of my humble profession has it that if you would become an outdoor writer you must first acquire the three basic tools of the trade—a camera, a typewriter and a wife who works.

Like most adages, this one fairly reeks of truth. But it is not quite complete. One other thing you need is a hide as thick as an elephant's, for no matter what advice you hand out, somebody is going to growl about it.

Take, for instance, a recent article by Biff Lampton in which he advised sharpening up your hooks before you go after tough-mouthed tarpon. Given the third degree, Biff would probably come clean and admit that he is not the first writer to suggest such a thing. In fact, that selfsame recommendation can be found lurking among the crashing leaps and screaming drags of virtually every fishing writer from the time of Izaak Walton to the present day.

There are sundry reasons why writers continue to carp about sharp hooks. For one, there is always the faint hope that some fisherman—someday, somewhere—might actually take this advice to heart and decide to start sharpening his hooks. For another, it's the only subject an outdoor writer can comment on without being challenged by someone who knows more about it than he does. Or so we used to think.

Biff may not be the first authority to espouse the philosophy of sharp hooks, but he is surely the first to catch hell about it from a reader. The hook of a tarpon fly should *never* be sharpened, this reader complained. To the contrary, the point should be clipped completely off. Why? So that the hook cannot possibly get stuck in a tarpon's mouth and perhaps remain there forever if the leader should break.

Of course, our correspondent was speaking from the narrow viewpoint of his own personal approach to small-tarpon fishing. Realizing this, I was just going to let the whole affair drop, but then it hit me that there might be two sides to many angling rules that we have long held as gospel, and that perhaps we outdoor writers are guilty of not exploring the flip side before we start handing out reckless advice.

I blush to recall, for instance, that just an issue ago I was exhorting you to use 100 per cent knots so as to land more prize fish. But maybe that's not such a good idea. To be honest, 50 per cent knots will make it much easier to get rid of the unwanted things that you hook far more often than big fish—things like snags, rocks, moray eels, mudfish, sting rays and your fishing buddies.

Boating writers, too, should pause before repeating their oft-issued warning to make sure your line is firmly tied or cleated before you toss over the anchor. Perhaps you should leave the anchor unfettered, especially when you toss it into deep water. Otherwise, you might have to haul the heavy thing up again—much to the delight of your neighborhood chiropractor.

We'll try to be more well-rounded with our advice in the future. Meanwhile, Biff and I are working on a hook-dulling machine that you'll soon be able to order at a bargain price from this address.

Vienna Sausage Fights Back

You may remember Miami's Great Vienna Sausage Bust.

Dade County officers closed in on a hot day last August to clamp the long arm of the law on one Quentin Jinks, age 19 months. The suspect was apprehended in the act of eating a Vienna sausage aboard a Metrorail car in flagrant violation of county law.

Determining that he was a juvenile, the arresting officers let Quentin go with a stern warning to keep his mouth shut on Metrorail thereafter. However, they confiscated the offending sausage and brought charges against his mother, whom they cited for contributing to the delinquent behavior of a minor: to wit, aiding and abetting the demi-toothed devastation of a Vienna sausage in a no-eating zone.

Ordinarily, we leave the reporting of criminal matters to the daily press—which did, in fact, cover the Jinks story as thoroughly as the ants covered what was left of poor Quentin's Vienna sausage.

But we cannot pass this incident off as just one more sad example of a young person who, mesmerized by the euphoric appeal of some irresistible substance, has strayed briefly from the path of righteousness. Insidious forces, we fear, may be using the Quentin caper as a weapon with which to attack the very foundations of sportfishing through one of its most beloved institutions—the Vienna sausage itself.

Brilliant minds have researched the long history of this association and are in general agreement that without Vienna sausage sportfishing may never have been invented at all, and certainly would never have prospered. Computer-generated graphs dramatically disclose virtually identical growth patterns for participation in recreational angling and sales of Vienna sausage. That both precisely parallel the astounding expansion of the antacid industry is considered an interesting, though insignificant, coincidence.

So deeply ingrained is the angler's dependence on these tasty little morsels that one distinguished scholar was moved to proclaim, in a widely read treatise:[1] "The three most basic needs of any fisherman are beer, insect repellent and Vienna sausage."

Imagine, then, the widespread concern among the fishing populace when a Miami newspaper reporter, commenting on the Quentin case, referred to Vienna sausage as something that shipwrecked sailors might eat "if raw seagull was not available."

That sort of unwarranted slur can but reflect upon the culinary naivete of the reporter, who obviously has never been privileged to sample the gourmet thrills hidden in the typical fisherman's luncheon.

For the benefit of that reporter, and all others similarly deprived, we pass along the most celebrated of all Vienna saugage recipes,[2] created by an unchallenged expert in this field:

"Remove lid from can and drain liquid overside, taking care that it does not come in contact with the boat hull, as it may dissolve aluminum or gelcoat. Use brace and bit to remove first sausage from can. Discard. Remaining sausages may be served to those aboard who have taken Dramamine."

1. Waterfront View, Florida Sportsman, Vol. 12, No. 1, Jan, 1981.
2. Op Cit, Vol. 10, No. 10, Oct., 1979

Yakkety Yak!
(Don't Talk Back)

O ptional at extra cost, you can get a car these days that talks to you. Some of that extra cost is money, but most is aggravation. The car doesn't just talk. It scolds. "Your . . . Lights . . . Are . . . On," it admonishes in a maddeningly patronizing tone just as you open the door amid a giggling crowd of bystanders.

Ours may be snootier than most talking cars, but it also unleashes its sepulchral lectures whenever we: leave the keys in the ignition, even for a moment; neglect to fasten our seatbelts; fail to close a door securely; or pass a gas station without stopping. And, who knows what other tongue-lashings it has yet to deliver?

This babbling option is listed on the window sticker of some new cars as "ABSD" (Automatic Back Seat Driver), and on others as "EN" (Electronic Nag). Married people do not really need this accessory but may end up with it anyway just because the car they pick out happens to have been infected with it at the factory.

When talking boats arrive on the scene—and they could be on the way right now for all I know—I predict a massive rise in the number of bridge fishermen.

The electronic voice in your boat will, of course, need its own private power source, since the bulletin it will broadcast most often (about half the time you turn your ignition key after launching) is:

"Your . . . Battery . . . Is . . . Dead."

And whenever you toss over the anchor you will have to live in dread of hearing this commentary:

"Your . . . Rope . . . Is . . . Around . . . Your . . . Ankle."

Somewhere in the middle of that, probably between "Around" and the second "Your," there will come a loud splash. Vehicles enunciate clearly but they don't get the message out very fast. I know because of something my car told me one day when I parked to eat lunch on a trip out of town:

"Don't . . . Forget . . . Your (sound of a locked door slamming) . . . Keys."

Thanks a lot, pal.

So, in your talking boat, you can expect to hear, sooner or later, a loud and sudden thump, followed by—as you try to back your head out of the windshield:

"Your . . . Hull . . . Is . . . Aground."

A vehicular voice, whether on land or sea, can always be depended upon to smack you with its worst news just when you're in the best mood.

For instance, after playing a big fish on light tackle for several hours and finally bringing it to boatside, you would expect to invoke some electronic cheering. Instead, you would probably hear:

"Your . . . Line . . . Is . . . Tangled . . . In . . . The . . . Propeller."

In case I ever get a talking boat (I don't expect to, but then I never dreamed of having a talking car either) I have already mapped out a last-line defense.

One day, while the boat is sliding off the trailer, it will say (with a faint tone of alarm, I hope):

"Don't . . . Forget . . . The . . . Plug." (Glug, glug.)

A boat can always be salvaged. But a mind is a terrible thing to lose.

A New Way to Skin a Cat

The reference to illegal netting of large redfish in this column concerned a highly publicized case in which a member of one of Florida's leading commercial fishing families was fined $500 for hauling in 35 tons of redfish that were larger than the maximum size limit.)

I have long speculated that the three best ways to get rich quick would be to smuggle dope, rob banks or open a health food store, but lately I've noted a couple of other endeavors that seem at least equally rewarding. In fact, one of them—the netting of illegally large redfish—appears to be a caper which grosses more than the average bank job, even though carrying no risk of meaningful punishment.

So far I have restrained myself from wandering any such primrose path, but now I am sorely tempted by an offer that promises rewards more fabulous than any of those others. True, a $50,000 investment is required but I have no doubt that bankers will be pounding on my door, money in hand, once they study the following prospectus sent me by a reader in Valdosta, Georgia.

"I have read a lot about your fishing exploits and know something about how much it costs to go fishing, so I thought I would let you in on the ground floor of a very profitable business I am setting up in South Georgia—a cat farm. We plan to start small with only one million female cats and one tomcat, so at the current market value of five cents per adult cat, your investment would be a paltry $50,000.

"Each female cat will average about 12 kittens per year and the skins will be sold for an average of 30 cents each, giving a gross revenue on 12 million skins of about 3.6 million dollars a year, or $12,000 per day, excluding Sundays and holidays.

"A good Georgia skinner could skin about 200 cats a day at a wage of $26. We will need 200 skinners, so the net profit will be $6,800 per day. Thus your $50,000 investment will be recovered in 7.35 days, which beats the hell out of playing the stock market.

"In the beginning, the key to operating successfully is that we'll have a rat farm adjacent to the cat farm, and will feed the rats to the cats. Since rats multiply four timers faster than cats, our stock of one million rats will be enough to feed each cat four rats per day. Conversely, one cat, after being skinned, will feed four rats. The cats eat the rats, the rats eat the cats and we get the skins.

"Eventually, the rat farm will be eliminated, along with all the threats made upon our lives by cat lovers, as we plan to cross the cats with snakes. They will skin themselves twice a year, which will also save labor costs and increase profits many times over.

"Until that time, however, our wives will have to help out by working in the rat house while you and I take care of business in the cat house.

"Knowing you are quick to recognize a good deal, I anxiously await your check."

I can't honestly say why this reader chose me to be his partner. I am a former resident of Valdosta, true, but that dates back to prehistoric times and cannot be the reason. His letterhead discloses that he is a polygraph specialist. Likely enough, he has a mania for truth and wanted to be sure of getting a truthful partner, so he simply selected the first outdoor writer whose name he ran across.

Food for (Preferably) Thought

While sportsmen are mightily upset at the havoc being wrought upon the stocks of breeding-size redfish by commercial fishermen in the Gulf of Mexico, we nevertheless admit a grudging admiration for the man who caused it all—chef Paul Prudhomme of New Orleans, creator of the dish called blackened redfish.

As any hunter or angler can tell you, it is no mean feat to take something of doubtful edibility, such as a bonito or armadillo, and convince our neighbors that they should not only serve it for dinner but thank us for it. In this talent, Prudhomme puts us all to shame.

The coarse, wormy, bloody bull red is one fish so ill-suited for food that no self-respecting sportsman would even attempt to foist one upon a mother-in-law, let alone eat it himself. Yet many people have been persuaded not only to eat blackened bull redfish but also (honest!) to pay for it through the nose. Prudhomme himself took time off from counting his black proceeds recently to comment that he is as mystified as anyone. Small reds he loves. Bull reds are about as appealing to him as raw kidney.

In looking for a silver lining to all this, an enterprising outdoorsman can nourish the hope that he too might be able to take some sort of basically obnoxious creature, sprinkle a handful of spices on it, set it on fire, give it a catchy name and make a few million dollars.

"Reddened blackfish," for instance, could be concocted easily from black sea bass coated with paprika and Tabasco. As to other possibilities, how about *Armadillo Alfredo? Gopher Stroganoff? Mudfish Mousse?*

The best candidate for success, in my opinion, would be *Possum en Papillote.* I base this choice partly on the name, which has a New Orleans ring to it, but mostly on the fact that a natural-born possum, without special treatment, is almost as unlikely an edible as the fillet of a bull redfish. Despite the beast's appearance, however, possum-eating is said to be almost a religion up north in Dixie where, as these celebrated lyrics attest: "Folks keep eatin' possum 'til they can't eat no more."

Obviously, if we could only discover what it is that

enables the folks up in Dixie to choke down their possum meat and sing about it besides, we could package the secret and sell it for ridiculous prices, as Paul Prudhomme does with his blackening mix.

One possible clue to the secret is the old myth which holds that before a possum can become—to use a gourmet term—"fitten to eat," it must be penned up and fed for a few days on clean food, such as Purina Possum Chow or the scraps from your own table. Great possum chefs throughout Dixie will keep a straight face and swear to you that the only reason for this is to purge the possum's system of the repulsive things he is prone to eat when foraging on his own. But that's what they *want* us to think. I have a strong suspicion that what they're really doing is pre-stuffing the possum with bread crumbs, onion, sage, celery and bay so that the chef need not bother to make the stuffing at all.

Pre-stuffed possums could become the culinary fashion in fine restaurants everywhere. For sure, they'd be easier to swallow than bull redfish.

Another Source of Lead Pollution

The following was written during a weird period in our history when the government allowed hunters with 16- or 20-gauge guns to fire lead shot at waterfowl, whereas those arming themselves with 12-gauge guns were required to use scarce, expensive and inefficient steel shot. This inequity has since been corrected. Steel shot—no longer scarce but still expensive and inefficient—is now required for everybody.

For several years now, a campaign has been under way to protect ducks from the toxic effects of 12-gauge lead shot, which presumably is more poisonous than the same shot fired from 16- and 20-gauge shells. The value of this campaign has been loudly debated in hunting circles since its inception, and no doubt will continue to be argued for years to come, inasmuch as the only specifically measurable result so far has been a sharp increase in the sales of 20-gauge magnum shotguns.

Anyway, most waterfowl biologists seem confident that the mandatory steel-shot rule (for 12-gauge guns) is a scientifically valid move that is bound to reduce the amount of lead in ducky diets, with the results that flocks will be increased, hunters satisfied and shell manufacturers made prosperous.

Unfortunately, however, the flow of lead shot into our waters continues—from a source completely overlooked by waterfowl managers.

Bream fishermen by the uncounted skillion practice their art every spring and summer in the very same weedy waters where duck hunters build their blinds in late fall. And has but lately come to the attention of embarrassed game officials that nearly every one of those bream fishermen pinches one or more lead shot haphazardly to his line, and that huge numbers of the shot fall off into the water.

A crash study, conducted with the utmost secrecy, has been mounted to determine the potential toxic impact of fishing shot—as opposed to, or possible in combination with, spent lead shot from shotguns. Information from this study has been leaked to us from a source we will protect to our dying breath.

Already the study has shown the problem to be serious indeed. While it's true that split-shot sinkers are not strewn over the lake in the dense patterns of shotshells, it has been demonstrated that there are many times more bream fishermen than duck hunters, and that they spend thousands more man-days on the water. Even though they drop only a few shot each trip, and those accidentally, the amount of lead deposited by anglers is computed to be nearly identical to the amount for which hunters are responsible, give or take a few million pounds either way.

Moreover, the loss rate for split shot is increasing dramatically because of a sharp rise in the average age of bream fishermen, this being due to the fact that once a canepoler begins wearing dentures he no longer is able to clamp his sinker as firmly to the line.

Even given the study's rush nature—and taking into account the government's established margin for error in fishery and wildife studies (80 to 85 per cent)—those are alarming figures. Something must be done, and the solution, we are informed, has been proposed in a memorandum from the Secretary of the Interior to the chief of the U.S. Fish and Wildlife Service, with copies to the heads of all state game agencies.

It is urgent, says the memo, that the use of split-shot sinkers be immediately banned on 12-pound lines, although they will still be permitted on 20- and 16-pound lines.

Sinker manufacturers, advised that the ban is forthcoming, have sought guidance on pricing from shotshell manufacturers, and have just announced that they will offer split steel shot by next spring. The price will be $3.98 for six shot, packaged attractively in a plastic bubble.

The Art of Short-Line Nymphing

Despite an ever broadening array of high-technology tackle, the ancient and honored cane-pole remains the overwhelming favorite of Florida bream and speckled perch fishermen. Age and economic status have little to do with it. When the bream or perch are biting, you see as many canepoles in gnarled hands as chubby ones; as many pole-carriers mounted on late-model Cadillacs as on vintage Volkswagens.

Pole fishing is great fun for all and, in most pan-fishing circumstances, deadly effective. This cuts no ice with flyrod purists—particularly some of those who inhabit northern streamsides. While they may acknowledge the effectiveness of canepoling, they stoutly refuse to recognize it as a gentleman's way of fishing.

For one thing, they hint darkly, it is atavistic. For another, it is far too easy. You can take a canepole and proceed to catch a bream with it (or even, heaven forbid, a hallowed northern trout) without first spending two years of practice and $500 for casting lessons—not to mention months of library research on such subjects as fly-tying, entomology, pipe-puffing and eyebrow arching.

Flyfishing for trout on small streams is more than a sport, more than a religion. It is a demanding science in which one pits his brain and equipment against a flood of biological phenomena, all conspiring to prevent the angler's feathered hook from coming in contact with the mouth of a trout.

After evaluating these various phenomena, the angler may use dry flies or wet, terrestrials or nymphs, streamers or muddlers. And sometimes the only hope of catching the trout is to throw him something so outrageously unlike anything he ever saw that he involuntarily opens his mouth to laugh, at which time the weird fly—called an attractor—is artfully retrieved so that it foul-hooks him in the corner of the mouth.

Of all the specialized flyfishing skills, there seems

to be general agreement that one of the most difficult is nymphing. In this approach, a scraggly fly representing the juvenile stage of an aquatic insect, must be fished deep, with a delicate touch and a near supernatural "feel" for the take.

Sometimes, ordinary nymphing techniques are not enough. I recently read an article in a national magazine in which the author described a highly advanced technique called "short-line nymphing." This must be resorted to when the trout are lying smack on the bottom of pools in small streams, refusing to rise even a little bit. They are able to get away with such uncooperative behavior because scads of natural nymphs are tumbling along the streambed right into their waiting mouths.

Plain old nymphing procedures cannot work because the fly does not sink fast enough, nor stay deep long enough. But flyfishing's vast body of expert lore contains an answer for every piscatorial problem.

The solution to this one is to use a short line, and to pinch one or two split shot onto the leader. The angler then flips out a short upstream cast, extends his rod parallel to the water at waist level and follows the course of the bouncing sinkers with his rodtip, from which the line hangs vertically. After the bait has travelled a dozen or so feet downstream, the angler raises it from the water and flips it upstream once more to repeat the process.

A master flyfisherman, given enough practice time, can become as adept at this technique as a Florida bream fisherman with a canepole.

Well, almost.

Time Is Billfish

A government survey of billfish tournaments held throughout the Gulf of Mexico, western North Atlantic and Caribbean Sea disclosed that it took 77,000 man-hours of trolling to produce 3,251 billfish. They were mostly marlin, since marlin were the principal tournament targets. Had there been more concentration on sailfishing the expended time likely would have been much less—probably 70,000 hours.

The embarrassing fact remains, however, that tournament billfishermen—who are the most avid of anglers and the best-fixed for boats, crews and tackle—were able to come up with only one billfish for every 24 hours of trolling.

And if you think that means a fish a day, think again. Actual trolling time in a tournament does vary, depending on the tournament schedule and the distance to the fishing grounds, but the average actual fishing time is about six hours a day. Thus, one billfish every 24 hours really adds up to one every four days, a span which equals or exceeds that of many tournaments.

To put it as kindly as possible, this is not a very good effort-to-success ratio. Still, tournament anglers are probably grateful that the government statisticians chose to billboard their ineffectual efforts in terms of hours rather than money.

Anyway, the need for improvement is obvious. Even more obvious is the fact that anglers, crews and manufacturers are all barking up the wrong tuna tower in their efforts to maximize efficiency. Their approach is to increase the catch, which they hope to do by developing can't-miss strategies, molding irresistible lures, designing sophisticated new instruments and building boats that raise fish better.

It should be evident by now that even if all that stuff works, increasing the catch is the slow road to improved efficiency, for even if they manage to *double* the catch, they'll still have to spend two days of aimless meandering in order to capture one marlin.

The logical approach, then, is not to up the catch but to pin down that one specific hour out of 24 when the angler will take his fish, and to stay ashore the rest of the time.

If this were possible—and who's to say what's possible anymore—think what it would mean to the time-pressed executive who likes tournament fishing. During close-to-home tournaments he could devote many extra hours—days, even—to his business, leaving the office just soon enough to make it out to blue water in time for his appointed hour with the marlin.

And when competing at distant locales, anglers would be able to spend most of their time at art museums, folk dances and other cultural attractions that make up a typical tournament social schedule, rather than having to spend 23 idle hours out of 24 watching plastic baits hiss though angry whitecaps.

The challenge will be in developing the instrument of prediction. A crystal ball would seem ideal, but I have examined several of these and, although I spotted a snowstorm in one of them, I found visions of striking marlin in none. Obviously nobody has yet come up with a crystal ball in a fisherman's model.

But in another direction, there are so many scientific wonder instruments on tackle counters these days that you know it's only a matter of time until some sort of electronic marlin-strike-forecaster is invented.

Somebody will probably figure it out during a billfish tournament, when he has plenty of time on his hands and nothing much to do.

An Explosion of Consumers and Taste

According to the chief lobbyist for the commercial fishing industry, Florida's population currently stands at about 250 million people, which is a neat trick, since that is more than the population of the entire United States. Teachers everywhere will be astonished to learn this, but grateful for having it pointed out.

The startling revelation came in a letter written by the aforementioned lobbyist to the director of the Florida Marine Fisheries Commission, in which he stated: "There really are a hundred times more consumers than anglers." Ordinarily, one might consider this a figurative comparison, but the emphatic "really are" indicates he is speaking literally.

Since the National Marine Fisheries Service reports that some two and a half million residents of Florida go fishing, it follows that our current population must be 100 times two and a half million, or 250 million. Of course, the lobbyist might have been referring to the whole country. If so, we must multiply 40 million (the number of anglers nationally) by 100, which gives us four billion residents of the United States. China beware!

All this leads to the question of how many consumers are consumers of fish, anyway.

Strange as it may seem to us fish lovers, great masses of consumers cringe at the very idea of eating fish, except for maybe canned tuna. In fact, members of the consuming public are frequently heard to exclaim, "Yuck. This fish tastes *fishy.*"

Executives of Church's Fried Chicken were well aware of the public's anti-fish-taste attitude when recently they decided to add fried catfish to their menu, but they were confident that their advertising geniuses could circumvent public resistance. And so they did. Featured in Church's catfish advertising is this reassuring promise: "Always delicious and never, ever fishy."

Because sales of Church's catfish are booming, other ad agencies are said to be planning similar campaigns for their own fast-food clients, using slogans such as, "Always delicious and never, ever hamburgery," or "Always delicious and never, ever pizzaey," or "Always delicious and never, ever tacoey."

Church's itself will probably attempt to boost sales of its basic product by proclaiming its fried chicken to be, "Always delicious and never, ever chickeny."

There have been other attempts to conceal the fishy nature of fish from a less-than-adoring public. The latest, of course, is "blackened redfish," which overcomes buyer resistance first with a catchy name and then with a coating and method of cooking that wipe out the last vestige of fishy taste by the simple means of cremating the consumer's taste buds.

If one of your favorite dishes happens to be jalapeno peppers that have been slathered with horseradish, dusted with chimney soot and run through an incinerator, you might also like blackened redfish. And if you do, I have good news for you. You need never be out of it, even when redfishing is closed. That's because the dish tastes exactly the same whether you make it with a redfish, a grouper, a jack, an ocellated frogfish or the tongue of an old tennis shoe.

Just heat and enjoy. The heating is the easy part.

In Search of . . . Catfish

One column ago I expressed surprise at the slogan adopted by Church's Fried Chicken to advertise its catfish: "Always delicious and never, ever fishy."

What surprised me was the fact that a restaurant would attempt to create mass interest in a new offering by issuing a written denial that it tastes like what it's supposed to.

Personally, I like catfish very much—provided that it tastes like catfish. Church's claim to the contrary was almost enough to discourage me from trying their new offering. But there were burning questions I couldn't leave unanswered. For instance, had Church's managed to steal Mrs. Paul's secret process for rendering fish tasteless?

And if they had succeeded in taking the fish out of catfish what, then, would the remainder be—cat?

Determined to find the answers, I went to lunch one day at Church's, and almost got cold feet the moment I walked through the door. Over at a corner table, several youthful employees were on break and nibbling at their own lunches—which came out of bags decorated with golden arches.

When I ordered the catfish, I thought I spotted a look of desperation in the attendant's eyes. Turning, she walked past the warming trays—from which customers ahead of me had been getting their chicken dinners almost instantly—and continued on past the frying baskets to disappear through a stainless steel door in the back of the shop.

About five minutes later the door coughed her back up—empty-handed. Ignoring an assortment of impatient remarks and exasperated sighs from the people in line behind me, she headed for the table where the off-duty employees were enjoying their Big Macs, and whispered something into the ear of one I assumed to be the shift manager. He got up and they both hurried through the enigmatic door. When they emerged several minutes later, she was carrying a tray of breaded fish.

From that point, it took only three or four minutes for her to fry the fish, make up my plate and hand it across the counter.

Fifteen minutes had gone by since I placed my order, and now I had new mysteries to contemplate. What had gone on in that back room? Had the boss been summoned to give catfishing instructions so the fish could be caught from a pond out back? Or was there a fish-taste-removing machine back there which only he knew how to operate?

And what about the jalapeno pepper which, according to the overhead menu, is included with every catfish plate? Was it there to cauterize one's taste buds just in case an errant wisp of fish taste had slipped past the inspector?

I'll admit that I didn't solve all the puzzles. But I did answer the *big* question, which was: Does Church's catfish taste good (meaning fishy) like catfish should?

In a word, yes. Much better than fish from any other fast-food chain, including those that specialize in seafood.

Slower too.

Anyway, while I was waiting for my catfish to emerge from behind that big door, I had time to think up a great advertising idea, which I herewith offer to Church's for free, just in case they are hoping to develop a TV commercial with as much impact as their print ad's witty words, "Never, ever fishy."

They could have this tough-but-lovable little old lady, see? And she could be glaring up at the counter after a 15 minute wait and demanding to know:

"Where's the catfish?"

No WhamRod?
Eat Your Heart Out

Little did I suspect, as I opened the envelope, that it held an invitation to join an exclusive— perhaps even snobbish—group. But there it was in black and white: I was one of a proud few (a mere million) selected to participate in a nationwide promotional campaign by paying only five dollars for that marvel of fishing technology, the WhamRod.

The formal name of this masterpiece is "Famous Nationally Advertised 660/F Telescoping Whisper-Cast WhamRod." However, as one of the chosen, I feel entitled to refer to it in the familiar form—WhamRod.

Some of you readers out there were similarly honored. As to you others, I don't want to rub it in, but how can one remain modest when he is about to own a WhamRod?

To be sure, some of its listed material are everyday stainless steel and aluminum but the WhamRod also contains "space-age fiberglass." Whether this futuristic material is to be found in the blank or the guides (or both), I am unable to say until the WhamRod reaches my quivering hands. No matter, I don't wish to seem picky and risk having my name stricken from the list.

A possibly unique feature of the WhamRod is that it is "at home on virtually every lake, stream or waterway in America."

Part brute and part pussycat, it is designed for "casting powerfully over long distances," yet it allows "Precise placement of small flies with a minimum of surface displacement."

That's quite an accomplishment, considering that the WhamRod is a spinning rod and one which measures "a full standard 66 inches from base to tip."

I am greatly excited, because I have hitherto been

able to cast small flies only with a flyrod, and not always with "minimum surface displacement." My failure to accomplish this with spinning tackle may well be due to the fact that none of my many spinning rods are of the "standard" 66-inch length.

If you're after drag-race performance take a look at this! The WhamRod "springs to complete length (and that's a full, standard, 66 inches, remember) in an eye-blinking 6/10ths of a second!"

That is probably a record time. No doubt, experts such as Lefty Kreh and Chico Fernandez could spring their WhamRods to complete length in perhaps 4/10ths of a second or less. But this we may never know, for Lefty and Chico may not have been included in the select list of one million.

Now don't go looking for a WhamRod in the store. You simply will not get a WhamRod unless you are among the chosen million, and even then you cannot buy one; you will have to send in a "Publicity Request Form," and not an order blank. The "giant multi-million-dollar New York firm" insists on this minor subterfuge, no doubt to keep WhamRods out of unauthorized hands.

If your name was not on the select list, there remains one small hope. Luckily, I read the small print and discovered that "there is a limit of two (2) rods at this publicity price, but if your order is mailed early enough you may request up to five."

So if you're the first to ask me about it, I might have a spare WhamRod to sell you. But not for any measly five bucks. You missed the publicity offer. Don't come to me unless you're ready to play hardball.

Improve Your Fishing Vocabulary

The English language is a particularly rich one, thanks in main to countless contributions made to our vocabulary over the centuries by peoples of diverse tongues and cultures. Although many of our word sources have been precisely traced, it is strange (perhaps even a plot) that those which derive from the sport of angling have been largely overlooked. One does not have to be an etymologist, or even a word expert, to see that many common words have their roots in fishing, even though their definitions have long since been corrupted to entirely different meanings. Here are a few examples:

BAS-RELIEF (originally bass-relief)—The sanitation device found aboard a bass boat, being sometimes a portable potty but more often an ordinary bucket.

BASSINET—A small net used to land juvenile bass, the larger ones being landed by hand.

BASSOON—The deep, rhythmic, repetitious reassurance by your guide that the bass will begin biting shortly.

CASTANET—A net thrown by hand, said to have originated in Spain, where it was used to catch both fish and certain large, colorful shorebirds called flamencos.

CASTRATE—A common measure of angling effort, referring to the number of casts made per hour.

DEBATE—What a fish does frequently to a sharp hook and routinely to a dull one.

FOUNDLING—A ling (cobia) spotted at the surface by an angler after a long and boring search.

HOOKY—The art of avoiding school in order to go fishing.

HOOKWORM—Any of various earthworms or caterpillars that will fit on a fishhook.

INKLING—The black color phase of a ling.

LINEAR—A medical term describing the ear of a novice flycaster and the line dangling therefrom.

MONOGRAPH—An elaborate graph traced with monofilament line between overhead power wires above a bridge.

POLAR BEAR—A species of bear which, having proven incompetent at catching fish in the manner of other bears, has resorted to using a fishing pole.

RED TAPE—The body of regulations applying to redfish in the Gulf of Mexico.

SPINOFF—The huge gob of snarled line that erupts from the spool of a spinning reel during the day's most critical cast.

SPINSTER—A woman whose interest in spinfishing is so all-consuming that she refuses to take time for courtship or marriage.

STARTLING—The first ling (cobia) to commence the annual run along Panhandle beaches in the spring.

A Great Invention
Strikes Again

Eight or 10 yeas ago, mail-order ads for electronic mosquito repellers lurked like leeches in the back pages of magazines. Nearly everybody bought one, and then stopped scratching only long enough to throw it away.

Recently, while digging through the mail, I was surprised to find that the Electronic Mosquito Repeller still lives.

Nostalgically, I read in the brochure that this little marvel "transmits middle audio frequency together with additional undertone and overtone frequencies." The logic, I assumed is that if you send out the entire range of frequencies, it is sure to include one pitch that is utterly abhorrent to mosquitoes— just as we might absently twist a radio dial until it happens to hit a heavy metal station and sends us into catatonic shock. Audio Russian Roulette, you might say.

But further reading of the literature disclosed that a deeper scientific principle is also involved.

"The electronic Mosquito Repeller," it explained, "simulates the sound of a male mosquito and since the mating cycle has been completed, the female is desperately trying to avoid the male." This, of course, is quite the reverse of human behavior, in which the female display of desperate avoidance takes place *before* the mating cycle.

Anyway, that's how the electronic repeller is supposed to work, but along with countless other optimistic outdoorsmen of years past, I painfully found that it didn't.

Perhaps the mating cycle of the mosquito isn't quite so predictable; perhaps all female mosquitoes don't come into season at the same time. Whatever the reason, as soon as I tramped into the woods and turned the thing on, millions of frustrated female mosquitoes, whose mating cycle obviously had not been completed at all, arose in a dense cloud and bee-lined toward the sexy male buzz that was emanating from the little gadget pinned to my shirt. Upon discovering that they had been duped by a vibrator, they immediately began exacting their vengeance in pints of blood.

Obviously, this instrument was not a repeller at all, but a caller. Since no widespread demand for a mosquito caller has ever surfaced, the gadgets gradually faded away, to lie dormant until their recent rebirth.

Years before that, I'd had a similar experience with another electronic device, this one a "fish caller." You were instructed to lower it into the water by means of a plasticized wire and then flip its switch, whereupon it was supposed to call in huge schools of fish from vast distances.

Testing the fish caller was easy in Dade County, where there are a lot of clear freshwater canals bordered by high, perpendicular limestone banks. I climbed to the top of one such bank and lowered the fish caller down among a group of small bass and bream that were lazing directly below.

As the cylindrical intruder sank, the fish all backed slowly away. When it stopped, a dozen of them approached to within a few inches, encircling the gadget and eyeing with curiosity. I threw the switch.

Scientists still debate the question of which fish are the fastest swimmers. Sailfish, marlin and wahoo are often mentioned as top speedsters, but none would have caught those six-inch bream and bass after my "caller" began to sound.

So the repeller calls and the caller repels. Hmm. If we just swap their packaging, maybe we could . . .

The Long and Short of It

Without any warning, a seven-foot jack crevalle suddenly jumped into the conversation at our hunting camp. The narrow path of credulity had already been greased by talk of a 60-pound bobcat and a flock of 75 turkeys but, even so, there was just no way a seven-foot jack crevalle could slide down it.

The jack, the wildcat and the vast crowd of turkeys all came from the same geographic location, that being the vast, mysterious and largely unexplored territory situated between the ears of our hunting buddy G.B. Snores (I'm not sure if that's the correct spelling, but there is no doubt of its descriptive accuracy).

As if he didn't realize that a seven-foot jack crevalle would be a monster every bit as horrible to contemplate (and just as fictional) as Godzilla or King Kong, G.B. swore that just such a creature had kept hijacking his hooked fish during a recent trip outside Boca Grande Pass on Florida's Gulf Coast.

What really rankled all of us in camp was that "seven-foot jack" kept slipping off his tongue without the slightest hesitation, as he maintained a perfectly straight face and a tone as smooth as honey. When I tried to repeat the words, my eyes bulged involuntarily and my voice cracked.

Try as we might, neither Biff Lampton nor I, nor anyone else in camp, could get G.B. to shave even an inch off his gargantuan fish.

In my sleeping bag that night I dreamed that Captain Ahab, contrary to the literature, had been snatched from the jaws of Moby Dick by a seven-foot jack crevalle, which then proceeded to swallow the captain himself, while the great white whale had no choice but to look on in helpless terror.

Next morning I walked into the woods with G.B. We parted company when I left the trail and headed toward a cypress pond, where I intended to take a stand.

On the way to the pond, I nearly stepped on a cottonmouth moccasin. This is a dangerous type of snake and normally I would have jumped out of my skin, but compared to the seven-foot jack crevalle that had been running around in my brain, it seemed innocuous enough.

The moccasin did, however, give me a brilliant idea. I would use it to trim G.B.'s fish down to credible size. This I would do by announcing in camp that I had seen a seven-foot moccasin. Even G.B. would have to protest mightily at such a brazen affront to truth. Cottonmouths occasionally reach five feet or so, I guess, but the only way you could come up with a seven-footer would be to tie two of them together with a uni-knot.

I rehearsed the plan in detail. This is what would happen: When G.B. questioned the length of my moccasin—as any man who cherishes honesty must do—I would immediately offer to take three feet off my snake if he would take three feet off his jack.

My searing humor would, of course, be met by thundering applause from all present.

The anticipated moment finally arrived. "G.B.," I said, "I almost stepped on a seven-foot moccasin down by the pond."

As he maintained a perfectly straight face, the answer slipped from his tongue without hesitation, in a tone as smooth as honey.

"Bad place," said G.B. "I see lots of seven-foot moccasins in there."

How to Snatch a Sasquatch

Some readers may by now have stopped quaking at the nightmarish visions of seven-foot jack crevalles, seven-foot moccasins and bobcats larger than tigers that prowled this space previously, thanks to the imagination of one G.B. Snores. I dislike exhuming what I hoped was a dead subject but unfortunately, Mr. Snores has seen fit to send a protest, which, in the interest of fairness and to avoid being sued, I pass along below for what little it may be worth.

"I read with interest your semi-accurate account of the seven-foot jack crevalle, the 60-pound bobcat and your own seven-foot water moccasin. I must point out a couple of errors and add a new report from those wild woods where we hunt.

"The jack, of course, does exist. I understand from the Boca Grande captains that this jack is becoming something of a legend in that domain of legends. They say the monster jack wrestles with Old Hitler, Boca Grande's famous whale-size hammerhead shark, for the largest and choicest tarpon on which to dine.

"The huge bobcat also exists. I'm sure many of your readers have seen the cat near the Lake Manatee Recreation Area in Manatee County. I suspect he grew so large because of his talent for frightening surprised bank fishermen away from their fish.

"As I told you, that swamp where you hunted is no safe place. It holds even greater dangers than your seven-foot moccasin. A Sasquatch, for one.

"It was my cousin, Jim Knowles, who first encountered the Sasquatch, known to some biologists as the Skunk Ape. It roared and chased him around that brushy cypress pond where you saw the snake. Jim (whose name, like mine, is spelled K-n-o-w-l-e-s, not S-n-o-r-e-s) never saw the beast but he smelled it and saw the trail it left in the swamp. Later, Jim's father-in-law, Ray Baden, not only saw the monster but nearly captured it!

"Baden was creeping about the gentle forest when he spied the Sasquatch sprinting through the underbrush. Clinging to its back were a number of bloodsucking bats. Ray gave chase and overtook the bigfooted hulk, which apparently was slowed by its loss of blood to the bats.

"Dr. I. Toleeso, in his famed treatise on Sasquatch infestations, notes that bats frequently parasitize these creatures. Apparently, according to the doctor, this is a symbiotic relationship, as the Skunk Ape is known to eat the bats during times of high water when game is difficult to catch. Anyway, Ray snatched at the Sasquatch as it raced through the palmettos, failing in his effort to snatch the Sasquatch only because his snatching hand closed over one of the bats, which he brought back to camp as proof of his strange encounter.

"You can be sure the Sasquatch is out there because several witnesses were sitting in camp when

Ray returned. A couple were outdoor writers, including Frank Sargeant of the Tampa Tribune, but there were reliable witnesses as well.

"The bat was a small one. Not over six or seven pounds, I'd say."

Never Trust a Set of Initials

The other day I met the president of the NFL but even before I could get around to mentioning Super Bowl tickets he let it slip that "NFL" stood for "Natural Flyfishing League."

This dedicated soul had been tying flies and fishing with them for many years. One day he was reclining on a grassy bank, mulling over the feathery contents of a little aluminum box, when he glanced toward the stream just in time to see a hovering insect disappear below the surface in a circle of foam.

This chance observation smote the astonished angler every bit as forcefully, if not so painfully, as the apple that once gravitated with a loud thunk upon the head of another prostrate visionary, Sir Isaac Newton.

Perhaps, he thought in a flash of insight, it would not be necessary after all to spend endless hours hunched over a vise tying gaudy and intricately patterned artificial flies. Had not his own eyes offered evidence that fish will eat the real things?

He began experimenting secretly—first with grasshoppers and crickets, then with horseflies, dragonflies and even such unlikely invertebrates as earthworms. All doubt vanished. Though certainly less artistic than traditional hand-tied artificials, natural flies and other insects really do catch fish!

In celebration of this milestone discovery, our hero founded the Natural Flyfishing League, unconcerned that the initials might already be taken. Membership is said to be mushrooming and the founder's niche in angling history seems secure.

The story of the NFL brought to mind another duplication of initials that once erupted on the Florida scene, shortly after the organization of the Florida Conservation Association.

In what they no doubt figured was a clever counter-measure, Florida's commercial fishing leaders got together and announced their own new group, which they called the Fish Consumers of America, or something like that. I forget the whole name but, anyway, "Consumer" was in there. And the initials, by strange coincidence, were "FCA."

Some unkind souls suggested that the commercials, miffed because the other FCA was being discussed so frequently and enthusiastically all over the state, had deliberately appropriated the same initials in order to create confusion in the public mind.

But there never really was any possibility that the two FCAs might get confused. They were easily distinguished by the fact that the FConservationA consisted of several thousand actual dues-paying members, whereas none at all could be found for the FConsumersA.

The FConsumersA ran into serious recruitment problems from the start. You see, people who shop for fish in markets tend to become instantly anti-social—if, indeed, not homicidal—upon being told the price of their purchases. You can imagine, then, the ruckus that must have occurred whenever one of these newly impoverished citizens emerged from a fish market, only to be accosted by a recruiter from the FConsumersA, suggesting that he dig even deeper into his depleted pockets so that he might join a fraternal organization of happy fish-buyers.

Many of the recruiters, we hear, recuperated nicely.

A Few Bird Books, Please, Santa

One recent bright June day, the postman brought me a copy of "Peterson's Field Guide to the Birds of Eastern North America." It was a Christmas present from my wife. Christmas of 1984. But this time the U.S. Mail was not to blame for the long delay.

I am not a dunce about birds but there are plenty

of them I can't identify, particularly among Florida's feathery transients. Cheryl knew I wanted a copy of "Peterson's" (I dropped the name just the way real birders do), and one day she spotted an ad soliciting subscribers for a whole series of Peterson guides.

What the heck, she figured. If I wanted one bird book I'd probably be delighted to get several.

For two and one-quarter years since that fateful decision, Mr. Peterson has been doing his best to bury us in books.

The first volume delivered was "Peterson's Field Guide to the Birds' Nests of Western North America." It was bound in leather and quite handsome—so long as it wasn't opened. Inside, it was full of ugly pictures of sticks and mud. But if you're going to collect, as Cheryl had said, "a few bird books," you do have to expect that some will be of only fringe interest.

Many months were to pass before I saw another book that had anything at all to do with birds. I received field guides to "Wild Plants," "Pacific States Wildflowers," "Mammals of Britain and Europe," "Rocks and Minerals," "Pacific Coast Fishes."

I actually opened "Peterson's Field Guide to Animal Tracks," in hopes of finding out what sort of creature had been walking on the hood of my car every night. However, I doubted that the culprit was a Canadian lynx, as suggested by the field guide. (An eyewitness later discovered that it was my very own cat, Kung Fu, whom I never would have suspected because he had direct orders to stay off the car.)

Peterson'ses kept coming: "Western Reptiles and

Amphibians," "Rocky Mountain Wildflowers," (not to be confused with "Pacific Coast Wildflowers"), "Pacific Shells." At last, the East got some representation, which raised my hopes sharply—"Eastern Reptiles and Amphibians," "Eastern Butterflies," "Atlantic Shells," "Atlantic Seashore."

A few I took to be universal in scope—"Trees and Shrubs," "Mammals," "Moths," "Insects." Then came a couple that *definitely* were universal—"The Atmosphere," "Stars and Planets."

Finally, the long anticipated "few bird books" began materializing, though far afield at first. I got "Birds of Mexico," then "Birds of Britain and Europe." I felt like celebrating when the good old U.S.A marched forth with "Birds of the American West" and "Birds of Texas."

The suspense struck a crescendo a couple of months back when I opened the carton and found "Eastern Birds' Nests." The pictures of sticks and mud looked the same as those in "Western Birds' Nests," but where there are Eastern nestlings, can Eastern birds be far behind? Sure enough, the next month it arrived—my long-sought copy of "Peterson's Field Guide to the Birds of the Eastern United States."

I could have turned off the flow of books at any time, of course, but old Peterson knows how to play a fish once it's hooked. Now I'm hanging in just to see how much natural history can possibly be left to cover. The next volume, I hear, is "Peterson's Field Guide to the Sea Slugs of the Northeastern Atolls of the Southwestern Pacific."

Fish Can Be
Gold-Diggers Too

A wise and venerable man once cautioned: "Wealth cannot buy love."

To which an equally wise and venerable—but much more practical—man responded: "True. But it certainly can rent a lot."

Through all the ages, humanity has been resigned to the fact that female people, in their quest for mates, frequently tend to favor men of substance over those of us who are merely personable and handsome. Now it has been disclosed that some female fish may feel the same way.

Girl wrasses will ignore even the handsomest and most virile males in favor of some wrasse nerd who happens to own a choicer piece of real estate.

According to Dr. Robert R. Warner of the University of California at Santa Barbara, the lady wrasse (pronounced "rass"—rhyming with "grass") picks out the plot that she considers the most ideally located in the whole bay area and then moves in to nest with whatever male holds title to it. Never mind that bigger, more vividly marked and more amorous suitors are clustered all about. Their holdings simply do not meet her standards. It's the pad she's after, not the guy who owns it.

To verify this materialistic attitude, Dr. Warner conducted an experiment in which he kidnapped the newlywed male and replaced him with a strange wrasse only two days after the nuptials had been consummated.

Did the female wrasse then dash about frantically, raising the salinity level with tears of grief over her missing husband? Not at all. She just yawned and welcomed the new guy to the hearth, complimenting him on his good taste in property and assuring him that prime landfront lots are sure to appreciate in value.

Though surprised, Dr. Warner was not exactly flabbergasted by such a shocking display of ichthyological materialism, having observed similar behavior previously in another fish, the freshwater mottled sculpin.

Nobody is worried about sculpins, but it's alarming to consider that female wrasses, by passing up the robust males and mating with punier ones who own more valuable property, are effecting the reversal of an ancient evolutionary process known as natural selection, or survival of the fittest. Members of succeeding generations of wrasses are in danger of growing smaller until eventually the last survivor will shrink away entirely, leaving only a footnote in some scientific journal—plus, of course, an estate as valuable as downtown Miami, with no one to leave it to.

When extinction occurs, certain wrasses will be sorely missed by anglers. While not particularly spectacular on the end of a line, some species, largely because of their delectable flavor, are highly popular. They include the California sheepshead, the tautog of the cold north and, of course, the showy hogfish of our own balmy reefs.

If you wish to catch as many wrasses as you can before they vanish from the sea, I offer one important bit of advice.

When you hook one, play it with extreme care.

Otherwise, you may lose your wrasse.

For Commercial Use Only?

During deliberations by the Florida Marine Fisheries Commission on the subject of possible gamefish status for redfish and trout, one commissioner voiced strong opposition to the idea of removing *any* species of fish from the commercial marketplace. This commissioner kept insisting that it would not be fair to limit a portion of the resource to recreational use.

Prodded by the MFC chairman, this commissioner readily conceded that, yes, he would also have voted against gamefish status for largemouth bass and snook, had he been accorded a chance to do so back when those species were placed on the non-commercial list.

Later, while I was chatting with this commissioner, he asked me: "If you should reserve a certain species of fish for recreational use, don't you think, in all fairness, that you'd have to set aside some other fish as strictly a commercial species?"

Well, no, I don't, actually. But because I have a mischievous streak in me, I would secretly love to see just how this would work.

First, of course, a commercial-only species would have to be decided upon (let's make it the mythical greenfish), and a rule written. I guess it would go something like this:

"No citizen of the state, nor any tourist, shall take greenfish for personal pleasure or consumption. Any greenfish taken must be sold or returned to the water."

Now, if greenfish happens to be one of your favorites, you have serious problems—but not insurmountable ones. Just make sure you always fish with someone else. Then, when you catch a greenfish you can sell it to your buddy in order to legalize the catch. And when he catches one, he can sell it to you. In either event, the sale and transfer must be effected immediately, for you never know but what a Marine Patrolman might be watching through binoculars.

Your big problem at the end of the day will be deciding which stringer to brag about—the one you caught or the one you bought.

If you happen to be fishing alone when you catch your greenfish, the only way you can keep it is to become a lawbreaker—at least temporarily. Try to smuggle the catch home. If you make it, you can sell the greenfish to your spouse and become a law-abiding citizen once more. You can go to bed with no fear of hearing sirens shriek toward your house in the middle of the night.

Things do become more complicated if you have friends over for dinner. There are two approaches you might consider—selling tickets at the door (including beverage and dessert, *prix fixe*), or submitting individual checks and charging for the greenfish according to the amount consumed.

As you pocket your earnings, you don a sorrowful look and tell your mother-in-law that you *have* to make her pay; it's the law.

There's a silver lining behind every cloud.

Confession Time:
A Knotty Secret

A dark secret has been seething inside me for several years now and conscience will not let me keep it any longer. The names have not been changed. Let the guilty be damned.

Once upon a time there was this big contest to find the best new fishing knot—a knot that would be quick and easy to tie and virtually as strong as the unknotted line. Naturally, the contest's sponsor wanted to make sure that the winning entry wouldn't be some little-known tie already in existence, nor one that was merely a clever variation of a standard theme.

The only way to make sure of these things was to get judges who knew all there was to know about knots, and then some.

So they got me, because I wrote a book that is half full of knots. And they got Lefty Kreh and Mark Sosin because they wrote a book that is *all* full of knots. Then, on the odd chance that Lefty, Mark and I might let a ringer slip past, they included famous national fishing experts Homer Circle, Jerry Gibbs and Ken Schultz, who may never have penned any knotty tomes but who have tied more and more varied knots than an epileptic octopus.

Fat chance that any knot known to history could slip by this authoritative gamut of eagle eyes!

We judges pawed our way through a mountain of submitted knots and finally we selected the winner—a little number that was simplicity itself, yet strong as could be. Best of all, it was totally unfamiliar to any member of the panel.

Nothing new under the sun, eh? Well, this knot was *new*. So said we all.

The winning knot was to be announced to a breathless public at a special ceremony the following day. Meanwhile, the judges would give a sneak preview of the knot that evening, during hospitality hour, for executives of the sponsoring company and for press and television people, including angling stars Roland Martin and Bill Dance.

The guests gathered 'round as I prepared to dem-

onstrate. At the far edge of the huddled group, ignored and standing on tiptoe to sneak a furtive
glance at the proceedings, were several wives. What
do women know about knots anyway?

My nimble fingers flew and the new knot was tied.
The onlookers uttered such comments as, "Ooh,"
and "aah," and "Well, I'll be darned."

The wives (mercifully) said nothing—at least not
until after the group had dispersed and only two or
three of the judges remained. Then my wife Cheryl
whispered, "That's a sewing knot. I use it all
the time." "That's right," said Carol, the wife of a
sponsoring executive, "I use it too."

My psychologist says it shouldn't bother me that
much. And it shouldn't, of course. After all, the knot
is a perfectly good one, and the sport of angling has
derived many of its standard knots from such diverse sources as sailors, surgeons, packers and
even hangmen.

But *seamstresses*?

I blush. Anyway, it's off my chest.

Get Set for Outdoor Olympics

Every four years, while watching the Olympic
Games on television, I am always amazed to note
that many of the athletic achievements extolled by

the announcers as near-legendary are actually much the same as feats that are accomplished routinely by fishermen, hunters, boaters and other lovers of the Great Outdoors. My chest swells with pride at the realization that outdoors people are at least the physical equals of other top athletes. My head swells also—with the idea of creating a special Outdoor Olympics just for them. Some of the planned events follow:

THE HIGH-LONG JUMP: Surprisingly, the Olympics not only separate this simple jump into two different events, but also allows a running start in each of them! Rare is the veteran hiker, hunter or bank-fisherman who has not surpassed both the Olympic High-Jump and Long-Jump records simultaneously, with leaps averaging nine feet up and 30 feet out—in a single bound and from a standing start. Of course, to duplicate that kind of performance in a stadium, the starter will have to press a button that unexpectedly sets off a loud rattling noise between the contestant's feet.

THE PUSHPOLE VAULT: Using a tubular fiberglass pole similar to an Olympic vaulting pole, the contestant—standing on the rear platform of a fishing skiff—will be allowed one hard thrust with the pointed end of the pole against a mud bottom. Score will be calculated on the basis of how far the vacated skiff advances, and how long the poler manages to cling to the stuck pole before sliding inexorably down into the goo.

THE ANCHOR THROW: Those few boating anglers who habitually ease their anchors over the side will not, of course, be in shape for this event, but most fishermen do stay in constant training and can be expected to heave 10-pound anchors for distances that will shame Olympic hammer throwers or shot-putters. The event will be held in two divisions, depending on whether the contestant's best throw was obtained with the anchor line loose or attached to the boat.

THE DOG HURDLES: As depicted on calendars, quail hunters and their champion pointers are featured players in an autumn tableau of grace and beauty. In the real world of the walking hunter, however, the dogs range within a shifting 100-foot circle, of which the hunter's boots form the hub. Unlike pantywaist Olympic hurdlers who need only clear barriers that are inanimate and evenly spaced, our competitors are constantly called upon to hurdle galloping dogs that materialize inches in front of them at unexpected moments. Those who succeed taste the thrill of victory, which they uncork back at the Jeep. Those who fail suffer the agony of defeat in a bed of brambles.

THE BALANCE LOG: Patterned after the Balance Beam event in women's gymnastics, our Outdoors Olympics version is more democratic, in that men and women may compete equally. The goal is to teeter one's way across a frigid stream on whatever thin and shaky log happens to be found. Competitors wear heavy jackets, insulated underclothing and five-pound boots, while carrying their choice of an eight-foot flyrod or an eight-pound shotgun: consequently, they are not required to display the all-around agility of those little Olympic brats who wear only a leotard. Even so, their dismounts are far more spectacular, usually consisting of three somersaults and two full twists followed by a loud splash.

Four years have passed since the above suggestions were first offered, without charge, to the Olympic Committee, which, incredibly, somehow neglected either to establish a separate Outdoor Olympics or incorporate the events into the next Olympic Games.

The Outdoor Pentathlon

An updated version of the Pentathlon seems the ideal event with which to cap the Outdoor Olympics announced earlier.

As everyone knows, the standard Olympic Pentathlon is a five-event competition devised in the 19th century to showcase the various macho talents of a dashing young cavalry officer, these being riding, cross-country running, swimming, shooting and fencing. The competition is based on a fictional scenario in which a prototypical lieutenant of cavalry is called upon to deliver a message to Garcia (or Hume-Fitzgerald or Lafayette or Von Bismarck, as the case might have been) across enemy territory. He starts out astride his charger, galloping like the wind and leaping all barriers until the gallant steed is shot from under him, whereupon he continues on foot at only a slightly slower pace, swimming rivers as required and intermittently decimating several platoons of enemy infantry through his skill with rifle and saber (or sabre, as the case might have been).

Since army officering, to put it bluntly, ain't what it used to be in Victorian times, the Pentathlon is obviously in dire need of updating. This is no small trick. But for our Outdoor Olympics, the challenge is made easier by the fact that the only present-day officer who is *ever* called upon—even in modified fashion—to exhibit the old skills of riding, running, swimming, shooting and fencing—is a game warden, or Wildlife Officer as they are officially called in Florida.

With this in mind, we have revised the Pentathlonic scenario as follows:

The Wildlife Officer is patrolling in his Jeep when he happens upon two men fishing from the bank. As the officer approaches to check their licenses, one man continues to cast nonchalantly but the other bolts to his own Jeep and scratches off in a cloud of dust. The officer follows in hot pursuit.

This is the *Riding* phase of the event. It covers hard road, dirt road, no road, stumps and sloughs.

Small deductions are made from the score for lost bumpers; large ones for lost axles.

When the Jeeps finally must halt because they no longer fit between the tress of a dense river swamp, the *Cross-country* phase begins. Points may be deducted here for hornet stings, twisted ankles and branch bruises on face and forehead. Then comes the *Swimming*. The officer must swim the oxbowed river twice just to stay in straight-line pursuit of the fugitive, avoiding alligators in the middle and snapping turtles along all shores.

Next comes the *Fencing*, which we have modified to mean getting across several barbed wire fences with alacrity, while losing neither patches of uniform nor chunks of flesh in the process.

And, finally, comes the *Shooting*. All cottonmouth moccasins encountered during events two through four must be neatly shot through the biting end with a service revolver before vice becomes versa. Needless to say, 90 per cent is a poor score in this portion of the competition.

Unlike that of the Olympic Pentathlon, our scenario has an ending. At length, the officer catches the fugitive and, gasping, asks to see his fishing license.

The man quickly hands one over.

"You have a license!" the officer screams. "Why were you running away?"

"Because *my buddy back there* didn't have a license."

Come to think of it, we may have to add a second shooting event.

My Answers: Completely Wrong

I picked up a big-name fishing annual published in New York that was fairly brimming with Q's and A's, and I couldn't resist trying to match my A's with their Q's, just to see how a hick fisherman from the backwaters might fare against the sophisticated angling gentry of Manhattan.

I flunked.

* * * * * * * *

Q: What is a speckled perch?

My A: A popular southern panfish.

Their A: It's a completely wrong name for a crappie, used only in the South.

* * * * * * * *

Q: Aren't restaurants wrong in listing "Walleye Pike?"

My A: They are if they don't have any.

Their A: Completely wrong! The walleye is a large member of the perch family and in no way related to the pike family.

* * * * * * * *

Q: Should a certain fish be called a bream or a bluegill?

My A: It should be called a bluegill if that's the kind of bream it is. Otherwise, it would have to be called a shellcracker, stumpknocker or redbelly, as the case might be.

Their A: The term "bream" is completely wrong. Bream are found in Europe, not the United States.

* * * * * * * *

Q: Are snook found only along the southern coast of Florida?

My A: There are plenty of days, months even, when they are not to be found on the southern coast of Florida.

Their A: Snook, also known as robalo, sergeant-fish, brochet de mer, and ravaljo, are widely distributed in the coastal waters of Florida, Texas, Mexico, Central America, the West Indies and West Africa.

My Q: But aren't at least a few of those names completely wrong?

* * * * * * * *

Q: Should I stock my pond with bluegills or pumpkinseed?

Their A: Bluegills are almost invariably preferred because they grow somewhat larger than pumpkinseeds.

My A: Try bream. They *all* grow larger than pumpkinseeds and some might grow larger than bluegills.

* * * * * * * *

Q: What's the right name of a fish called a lawyer?

Their A: The name is erroneously given to the red (mangrove) snapper.

My A: Completely wrong! Completely wrong! Completely wrong! A mangrove snapper is parenthetically confused with a red snapper only in the North. And particularly, no doubt, in northern editorial offices.

121

Blame It on Esko Honkala

You probably saw the ad in all the fishing magazines. Esko Honkala, who is the picture of an old-world craftsman if I've ever seen one, sits somewhere in a dark corner of the Rapala factory in Finland. He sits at a rough-hewn table on a rough-hewn floor next to a rough-hewn tank in which he tests flawlessly hewn Rapala balsa lures. The Finns obviously have better lure-whittlers than carpenters.

As the ad explains, old Esko will not be hurried. No matter how piteously American fishermen whine for more of his Shad Raps, old Esko sits at his little table, sipping now and then at his half-empty cup of cold coffee, twisting the eyes of Rapalas—a little bit this way and a little bit that. Then he pulls each individual lure through the tank with a little fishing pole. When he pronounces that one is properly tuned, another Rapala heads at last for America. It probably will clear the Atlantic more quickly than it cleared Esko Honkala's rough-hewn table.

Meeting Esko Honkala through this ad explained a lot to me. Finally I began to understand why the original Rapala plugs were so hard to come by back in the early '60s.

A famous story in the old *Life* magazine created immense overnight demand for Rapalas, and the thousands of anglers who managed to get some of the lures before the supply dried up had to admit that, for once, *Life* magazine knew what it was talking about.

The ensuing Rapala famine seemed interminable. Grown men would cry if they lost one to a bass. Unsavory sorts would rent their Rapalas (after getting a $50 deposit, of course) to poor addicted fishermen for five dollars a day. And that was during a time, remember, when five bucks was worth nearly five bucks. Anyway, sensational divorce cases were fought over which spouse would get the Rapala.

At the time, I wondered why Finland didn't just ship us a boatload or two of Rapalas. Russia was mad at us but I didn't think Finland was. We were getting all the fancy Sako rifles we wanted, why not a few Rapalas?

But how could I have known, back then, about old Esko Honkala? I can picture him now, though, sitting at that little desk, trying to see over a giant pile of untuned Rapalas, pawing through the lures in search of his coffee, muttering bad words about *Life* magazine.

It was along about then that I witnessed a sale in a small tackle shop at Lake Okeechobee. A tourist walked in, spotted four Rapalas in the display case and told the proprietor, "Sell me all four and I'll pay you $10 each!" He plunked down the 40, and after he had the lures safely in hand he chuckled and said, "I can sell these for 25 bucks apiece when I get back to Atlanta."

"I hope you can," said the proprietor, "but I doubt it. I *bought* those plugs in Atlanta just yesterday. You want more? I got plenty for $2.50 each."

I figured right then that the great Rapala drought was finally over. Some bright new sales manager had probably slipped pep pills into Esko Honkala's coffee.

The Rapala's vast following has never slipped, of course. Like most other anglers, I would hate to go fishing without a few in my box. A friend of mine expressed the general feeling about this lure pretty neatly one time, when rebutting someone's remark that the lightweight Rapala doesn't cast too well.

"I'd use it," he said, "if I had to train a duck to take it out for me."

Notes from an Editor's Mailbag

You are invited to wade with me, if you think you have the stomach for it, through some of the mail that crosses the desk of a fishing magázine editor.

The first thing here is a press release about a bamboo flyrod that's being imported from France to sell for $300 a pop. It is the unenviable task of the publicist to explain why anyone should pay $300 for a rod made of obsolete material. He makes a game try: "This ultralight rod," the release states, "is so responsive that the slightest flick of the wrist sends it where you want it."

There's the reason: you could send it out for a six-pack.

Ah, press releases. Here's another, from the Bass Anglers Sportsman Society. In it is a reference to Ray Scott, the society's affable founder. "Until Scott started talking about bass fishing, folks thought it was a pastime, an amusing recreation spent with a simple hook, line and sinker."

You sure anybody ever thought that?

A query letter is one in which a free-lance writer summarizes his idea for a story, and inquires as to the editor's possible interest in it. To help along his cause, he often includes a few words of self-praise. Here is an example from my stack of mail: "As a teacher, my writing has been of a professional nature for many years."

Another professional had a similar boast in another query: "My particular strength lies in writing."

Some writers skip the query letter and just send the manuscript. That's how an editor gets to read such prose as the following: "The big engine roared to life. 'Sounds like distant thunder in the belly of a seagoing dragon,' someone remarked."

To say nothing of the thunder such writing creates in the belly of an editor.

If you like puzzles, you'd enjoy reading some of these unsolicited works. For example: "Mother Nature and I are constantly in conflict when shallow water fishing. At times, even with polarized glasses to watch a fish easier, she would direct it to work into an area where light rays could not be controlled."

Near as I can translate, the author is trying to tell us that if you go fishing with Mother Nature while she is wearing polarized glasses, you should stick to areas where light rays can be controlled.

Many letters come in with reader requests. "Can you send some information," one asked, "on stripped bass?" Should I reply that the only bass I ever saw that *wasn't* stripped was a mounted one in an upstate bar? It wore a Florida Gator cap on its head and orange athletic socks on its pectoral fins.

Another reader wanted more detail on a point he had read in a past issue. "Would you care to elexcidate?" he inquired.

Sounds like it might be fun, but I've never tried it.

At the bottom of the mail stack is a copy of another state's outdoor magazine. On its cover is a blurb promising a feature article about a famous angler's "Water Elimination Method."

I didn't read the article. I'm satisfied with my own method.

Fishing Sitcoms Come to TV

At the time this column was written, America's beloved television bigot, Archie Bunker, had moved from "All in the Family" to "Archie Bunker's

Place"—his place being a tavern which (by some strange quirk of TV fate) Archie co-owned with a Jewish partner. At the same time, another comedy series, "M*A*S*H" (Mobile Army Surgical Hospital), was continuing its phenomenal run as one of the most popular television series in history. Naturally, such successes would spawn a rash of imitations.

From out in Televisionland comes word that a prominent producer is busily creating two new fishing shows for next season—not the familiar kind of pap that has been fed to us on weekend afternoons for these many yawning years, but prime-time dramatic programs with scripts written straight from the everyday trials and tribulations of America's anglers.

Here are previews of both shows, provided by the studio's publicity department:

* * * * * * * *

ARCHIE'S BUNKER PLACE—In this true-to-life program, the leading character, Archie, is proprietor of a bait and tackle store specializing in fresh bunker (a small species of fish widely used as bait and chum). Sundry comic characters hang around the place at all hours, but the chief source of humor is the fact that Archie is a bigot.

There are many kinds of fish that Archie simply cannot tolerate—red grouper, yellowtail, Spanish mackerel, cubera snapper and African pompano, to name a few. His personal favorites are whitefish, whiting, white perch, white bass and white marlin.

In the first episode we roar helplessly as Archie— mostly because he stubbornly refuses to stock what

127

he derisively calls "Jap tackle"—becomes strapped for cash and is compelled to take on a business partner. Only after he signs the agreement does he discover, to his chagrin, that his new partner is—get this—a jewfisherman!

In a succeeding episode Archie is taken aback to hear that his teen-age niece has a friend who is a black bass fisherman. Imagine the rollicking complications that arise as Archie frantically tries to determine whether the person in question is a black who fishes for bass, or an angler who fishes for black bass. In either case, of course, Archie will insist that the friendship be terminated.

Laughs galore every week, as fishermen join society's mainstream by learning bigotry.

* * * * * * * *

F*I*S*H—The initials stand for "Fishing Injury Surgical Hospital" but devoted fans will refer to this irreverent program simply as "FISH."

The protagonist is the irreverent "Gulleye" Pierce, a brilliant, dedicated and once wealthy surgeon who, ruined financially by a malpractice suit, has taken a position as Chief of Surgery of a F.I.S.H unit in order to pay his way through law school. His partner is Dr. "Funnycutt" Johntrapper, whose nickname derives from his nervous habit of doodling with his scalpel while operating.

These brilliant and dedicated but irreverent physicians use both slapstick comedy and cynical wit to combat the stress of running a field hospital for fishermen at a metropolitan marina, where they must face an endless parade of trauma victims. Con-

trasting the irreverent humor of the principal characters against the pain and suffering with which
they must deal every weekend, the camera spares no
bloody detail of such carnage as treble hooks dangling from human flesh; thumbs burned to the bone
by whirling reel spools; lockjawed mangrove snappers clinging to bleeding fingers; inflamed mosquito
bites; fourth-degree sunburn; catfish envenomation
and trailer-winch elbow.

Coast Guard helicopters drone constantly overhead, bearing emergency cases of seasickness,
alcohol overdose, Vienna sausage poisoning, acute
frustration and the many other syndromes common
to the weekend angler.

Be sure to catch F*I*S*H next season.

A Vote for the Hog Sucker

Co-written by David Dunaway

Fisheries scientists, it seems to us, are guilty of
discrimination in their selections of new species for
possible introduction into Florida waters. They look
only for the "beautiful people" of fishes, ignoring the
fact that most fish, like most folks, are not fashion
models or star athletes. It's nice to have a lake full of
striped bass, sunshine bass, peacock bass or wall-

eye—all of which have been stocked at least experimentally in Florida. But is it fair? Shouldn't those fancy kinds of fish be balanced by a few types that can boast nothing more than "good personalities," as they used to say about our blind dates.

Searching diligently through *McClane's Standard Fishing Encyclopedia,* we have found the perfect candidate to rectify this discriminatory stocking practice in our state. It is the northern hog sucker—a creature of exquisite grossness, but one which boasts certain other attributes, as we note below, with quoted support from *McClane' Encyclopedia:*

1. It is easily recognizable. "It has a large head with a depression between the eyes and a sucking type mouth."

2. It is punctilious. "Its preferred habitats are riffles and adjacent areas of clear, shallow streams with gravel bottoms."

3. It is prolific. "A biological survey team captured 130 hog suckers in a riffle area less than one-half mile long."

But it is also (4) careless. "Its eggs are not guarded and minnows rush in to feast upon them as they are laid." Which is just as well. Otherwise the biological survey team (see item 3) would never have been able to wade through a half-mile of habitat without being smothered by hog suckers.

Admittedly, the hog sucker's appeal as a sports fish is clouded by its feeding habits. "It uses its long snout and large head to turn over rocks. Food is obtained by sucking up the ooze and slime which is exposed when the rocks are moved." It will be devilishly difficult for angler seeking hog suckers to bait a hook with ooze and slime. Perhaps the ooze and slime could be mixed with cotton to provide hook-holding substance. Another possible solution would be to go down to the bait shop and buy some frozen ballyhoo, which turns to ooze and slime as it thaws.

But the point is not worth debating, since the hog sucker can contribute to the angling experience without being fished for itself. "As it roots a path, it is often followed by other fish, which feed on insects that are dislodged. The smallmouth bass is the game species most frequently observed enjoying this free board."

Probably we would not have to go to all the trouble of stocking smallmouth bass along with the hog suckers. Chances are, our native largemouth bass would also follow along after the hog suckers and so make convenient targets for our stream anglers. But if largemouth bass were involved, we would, of course, have to change the hog sucker's name to "hawg sucker."

We can tell you that it was no easy task to choose the hog sucker for stocking in Florida over many other fine suckers listed in *McClane's*. Among close contenders were the bigmouth buffalo sucker ("the largest member of the family"), the highfin carpsucker (virtually indistinguishable from the river quillback and plains carpsuckers"), the longnose sucker ("with a bulbous snout projecting far beyond the upper lip"), the webug sucker ("said to consume large quantities of trout eggs"), the lake chubsucker ("a greenish sucker without a lateral line"), the flannelmouth sucker ("distinguished by its unusually large lower lip") and the humpback sucker ("a grotesque-appearing sucker with a prominent pre-dorsal hump").

If you have some other nomination, feel free to send that sucker in.

Bring on the Walleyes—and Relax

M‌y wife and I were drifting across Lake Monroe, trailing tiny Beetle Spins on four-pound-test line. With pleasing regularity, a speckled perch would grab one of the lures and—in no more time than it takes to crank an ultralight spinning reel a couple of dozen turns—would come obligingly to the boat to join others on our stringer. Except for the fact that I was getting outfished by about four to one, it was a fine and relaxing trip.

But all at once, something definitely non-perch

grabbed Cheryl's spinner. It surged downwind and went under the boat. Cheryl, even while attempting to outsqueal the drag, managed to clear her line without touching the motor. But it was no use. The skimpy thread broke anyway, abetted by some tough or toothy mouth. It could have been a bass, a striper, a catfish or a mudfish. We'll never know.

Anyway, the intrusion was most unwelcome. If we had wanted to hook things that scream the drag, break the line and leave us trembling and scratching our heads, we would have gone fishing in the ocean. The great appeal of fishing for speckled perch (erroneously called "crappie" in the North) is that they seldom threaten to pull you overboard. When they're biting, you just sit there and haul 'em in.

The one thing that speckled perch lack is size. That's not much to give up in view of the quantity available but, still, wouldn't it be great if Florida had a freshwater fish that was both weak *and big*?

Actually, there is such a fish. It is well known over much of our country and may soon be well known in Florida, thanks to experiments by the Game and Fresh Water Fish Commission.

It's the walleye.

If you thought that walleyes can live only in much colder water than Florida has to offer, you thought like I did—until biologist Phil Chapman told me they can tolerate at least 85-degree water temperatures. They probably cannot spawn here though, which is all to the good, since biologists prefer to work with non-native fish on a put-and-take basis.

"We think the walleye might help us crop forage

fish, particularly in eutrophic lakes where there aren't many bass. Also, they grow large enough to prey on unwanted fish that are too large for bass to eat—tilapia, for instance. And, of course, it would be great if Florida could get a valuable predator that also broadens the angling experience for Florida fishermen."

As you may have noticed, there are anglers in Florida who originally came from somewhere else. Many of these used to fish for walleye—some exclusively, on the advice of their heart specialists. Chapman says these naturalized Floridians will be most enthusiastic about the walleye program.

And why not? Think of a fish that tastes even better than a speckled perch and, in my experience, pulls no harder, even though it averages several pounds in weight and can reach 10, or even 20.

So bring on the walleyes, I say.

But be aware that there is an occupational hazard. It is found only among anglers who fish for walleyes to the exclusion of all else, but it is still wise to be aware of it. It is explained for us by Cliff Shelby, who is a reverse hybrid—a former Florida resident who moved to Arkansas.

"Every now and then a walleye fisherman hooks an unusually large specimen. If the angler is using four-pound or six-pound line and has his drag set very lightly, the walleye may pull a yard or so of line off the reel, causing the drag to sound off momentarily.

"When such a thing happens, the walleye angler naturally thinks his reel is coming apart and he sends it back to the factory for overhaul."

A Reassessment
Of the Walleye

Perhaps I spoke a bit hastily a few columns back when I applauded the experimental stocking of walleyes in certain Florida lakes by biologists of the Game and Fresh Water Fish Commission. I admit that this was a somewhat impetuous endorsement, based on the dual considerations that walleyes seldom put an unsightly bend in your spinning rod, yet are among the elite of freshwater table fishes.

Now Charley Dickey, a well known outdoor writer and book author, has taken me to task.

"Vic Dunaway favors the stocking of walleyes," Dickey wrote in a column for the Tallahassee *Democrat*, "because cardiac patients can fish for them with no danger of blowing a gasket."

Dickey's personal feeling, however, is that much additional study is needed before we welcome the walleye to Florida with open ice chests.

"The walleye from cold northern waters is a delicacy that even a southerner raised on channel catfish can appreciate," he said, "but just how tasty a walleye from sub-tropical waters will be remains to be seen."

A related problem also worries Dickey. "Another unknown is how well a warm-water walleye will go with grits. Nor is there anything in the literature about the compatibility of warm-water walleyes and hush puppies."

I blushingly admit that this critic's points are all entirely valid. Moreover, I have since thought of another objection myself.

The walleye is—let's face it—ugly. We already have the mudfish and the gar to detract from the streamlined handsomeness of our largemouth bass (at least the younger ones who have not yet grown flabby-jowled and pot-bellied) and the colorful brilliance of our various species of bream.

With his bulging, glassy eyes and vacant stare, the walleye looks less like a fish than like a fisherman who has arisen at 5 a.m. in order to reach the water, in a semi-conscious state, by dawn. If that fisherman's first catch of the day happened to be a walleye, he would shudder and toss it back in disgust, thinking he had cranked in a discarded mirror.

Since my earlier column, I have received only two letters concerning the great Florida walleye experiment. One was from a transplanted Ohio native who has been living in St. Petersburg for four years. He wrote that when he first came to Florida he was concerned about having to give up walleye fishing. Then he caught a few redfish and trout and ladyfish and decided that the entire walleye clan should enroll in a physical fitness program.

The other letter was one that sought additional data.

"Is it true," a reader asked, "that a walleye fights like an old sock?"

I couldn't answer. He forgot to say what size sock.

Anglish Spoken Here

$\mathbf{W}$ho would think of taking a vacation trip to Mexico or France without a working list of common English-Spanish or English-French phrases?

For the newcomer to the strange world of angling, fishing talk is at least as difficult to comprehend as other alien idioms, and so for the beginner in the sport, and outsiders who may unwittingly fall into conversation with a fisherman, here are some of the most common Anglish phrases with English translations.

"My wife doesn't care much for fishing." Translation: "I used to take her but she always caught more than I did."

"I had a good one hooked, but a mackerel must have come along and cut my line." Translation: "I forgot to check my drag setting."

"The fish here always run along the edge; they don't get up on top of the flat." Translation: "If you think I'm going to pole around on that flat and look for fish, you're nuts."

"I caught plenty of fish but I let them all go." Translation: "Couldn't keep the catfish off my hook."

"I kept breaking them off. Then I checked my line and found out it was fatigued." Translation: "I haven't changed my line since the big discount house sale of '82."

"Sand perch are the best eating fish of all."

Translation: "That's all I caught."

"If ladyfish weighed 50 pounds, nobody would bother to fish for tarpon." Translation: "That's all I caught."

"A jack crevalle could pull any other fish backward." Translation: "That's all I caught."

"The bottom here has really changed since the last trip." Translation: "I forgot where the hole is."

"I'm thinking about going fishing Saturday, but I'll have to check my appointment schedule first." Translation: "I'll go if my wife will let me."

"I'd rather watch other people catch fish than catch them myself." Translation: "I got skunked."

"Two-pound bass fight a lot harder than the big ones," Translation: "I didn't get anything over two pounds."

"I just don't enjoy fishing with live bait." Translation: "I couldn't catch any live bait."

"The water was too calm." "The water was too rough." "The water was too clear." "The water was too murky." Translation (synonymous): "I didn't get a single hit."

"They say those gafftop catfish make great eating." Translation: "You try them and let me know how they are."

"This creek has always looked good to me but I've never fished it before." Translation: "What the heck creek is this, anyway? And where the heck is the one I'm looking for?"

"The main reason I go out is just to enjoy being on the water." Translation: "Maybe I'll catch something some day."

Sometimes a Great Lure

Some of my most pleasant and relaxing days have been spent with native bonefish guides in the Bahamas. The fact that they are efficient at their trade is almost secondary to their personal charm and dignity, their unpressured approach to fishing and their seemingly endless patience with even the most inexperienced or fumble-fisted angler.

The only thing that comes close to taxing the legendary patience of a Bahamian bonefish guide is an artificial lure. Tie on to the end of your line and, almost invariably, your guide's eyes will roll heavenward as he silently prays for divine protection from foolish gadgets.

But, being ever courteous, he is sure to find just the perfect words to let you know, softly but firmly, that if you throw that atrocity into the water, every bonefish for miles around will recoil in horror and bury his face in the sand. If you expect to catch a bonefish, he will advise pleasantly, you'd better get rid of the jig as quickly and secretively as possible, and bait up with a piece of conch or crab.

Over the years, I have had my artificial lures challenged by the best of guides throughout the Bahamas, in the most determined yet diplomatic of oratory.

My favorite of all anti-lure speeches was delivered by an elderly gentleman who guided me one day in the Berry Islands, By appointment, I met him one morning at a little dock on the backside of Frazer's Hog Cay, where I found him sitting in his skiff with his head buried in his hands.

It was obvious that he did not feel very chipper.

"I oversport meself last night," he confessed, adding that he was getting a bit old for that sort of thing, although he had been quite good at it in his youth.

His headache only got worse when he saw that my spinning outfit was rigged up with a bucktail jig. But even the pounding in his skull did not rob him of diplomacy. He held the lure between his fingers for a long minute, creating the impression that he was giving it a thorough and professional evaluation.

Finally, he said: "Dey tells me dat in Florida de bonefish bites dat. And I hear dat in Bimini *maybe* dey bites dat. But aroun' here, dey don't bites dat."

Knowing that my rebuttal had to be delivered as gently as his lecture, I suggested that I be allowed to try the jig on the first fish or two and then, after it proved ignominiously unsuitable, I would switch to bait.

I had not oversported myself the night before and was casting pretty well. My luck was good too, and the small fish we kept finding were hungry. As a result, I caught eight fish on the bucktail that morning. Using conch, my guide had not had a bite.

When we returned to the dock, he knew he must somehow acknowledge the effectiveness of the jig, yet do it without losing face.

"As I was telling you dis morning," he said, *"sometimes* dey bites dat."

Unrelated but Earth-Shaking Data

Here is a compendium of little-known facts and learned advice about angling:

—Never put leftover chum in your refrigerator. Next time you need it, you may find your wife has served it to her bridge club on Ritz Crackers.

—Suspicions verified: A leak at the National Weather Service (a news leak that is; they don't even count the water leaks) has confirmed that when the weatherman predicts winds of "five to 15," you can be sure that the "15" refers to wind velocity on the water and the "five" to the breeze behind the barn.

—The world-record flyfishing leader was tied in the Florida Keys in 1978 by Capt. Fred Nitrigger. It contained 11 tapers, two tippets, six Bimini Twists, eight other knots, 14 inches of decorative needlepoint and a yard of macrame.

—It is not true that a mangrove snapper will hold on to your finger until it thunders. Any loud noise will possibly make him turn loose. Try screaming at the top of your voice while simultaneously prying at the snapper's jaws with a large screwdriver. Neither tactic is apt to work by itself.

—During the past decade or so, and despite crowded waters and declining numbers of fish, participation in angling has risen dramatically. Contrary to popular belief, this phenomenon is not due to increases in spendable income and leisure time but to the fact that football saturation on weekend television has, for the first time in history, made it easy for a husband to talk his way out of the house.

—A world record was set this year at the Southern Open Bass Tournament when the winner, Lunker T. McHawg, became the first bass tournament angler to utter four consecutive sentences without once saying "structure," "pattern," or "flippin'."

—A new study of offshore trolling success discloses that, for all Florida waters all year, the angler can expect to average .258 strikes per hour of careful bait-watching and 3.67 strikes per trip to the head.

—It can be statistically demonstrated that deepsea fishing is the most demanding of all sports. Consider: A baseball player who goes to bat 100 times and gets 30 hits is a star. A quarterback who throws 100 passes and completes 55 is a star. But a deepsea fisherman who goes out 100 times and comes back 99 times is a has-been.

—Only a fisherman knows what it means to return home late at night, dog-tired, aching and sunburned, and find a smiling woman with a cold drink in her hand and some soothing words of sympathy. It means he's in the wrong house.

Fastest Rod in
The Gulf Stream

Did you think that fast draw is a talent useful only in old movies and those modern gunfights where the opponent is a stopwatch? Not at all. Competitive light-tackle fishermen in Florida have learned to draw and shoot faster than the eye can follow—flicking the button of a baitcasting reel or the bail of a spinner as adeptly as Wyatt Earp ever fanned a hammer.

Consider, too, that the gunman never has a multiple choice of guns from which he must instantly select the right one. He has only to sneer and draw—one gun from one holster. The competitive angler, by contrast, finds himself looking at a dozen or more "holsters" (he calls them rod holders) containing as many different fishing weapons. When a fish appears his challenge is to make the quickest judgment of the best lure or bait on the most appropriate outfit, then draw the chosen piece and fire out the first cast.

If he is a millisecond behind his boat buddies, he suffers a fate which to him is far worse than a bullet in the breadbasket. Somebody else will hook the fish.

Fishing clubs are the great training grounds of piscatorial fast draw. The typical new member arrives upon the club scene puffed with self-importance and eager for new fishing foes to conquer. He has soundly whipped everyone on the local piers and bridges and seawalls and headboats, and has no doubt he can do the same to those doddering 40-year-olds who sit at the club bar and recount great catches of olden days (the 1970s).

The carnage is terrible to behold the first time our novitiate accompanies a couple of club veterans out in their fishing machine. By the time he says, "Hey, guys, I think I see a . . ." it is already flopping in the fishbox.

"Sorry I had to do that to you kid," says the old-timer who caught the fish. "But better it happens now than in a tournament. You're fast, kid, but not fast enough yet for this kind of company."

Through continuing practice, raw talent is developed and polished. Next time out, the kid is at least reaching for his rod by the time one of his elders hooks up. Then, one day, his own rod is cocked for the cast just as his mentor's lure gets under way. It's close now, and only a matter of keeping the muscles toned up in the casting arm and developing the single-minded concentration necessary to send the hand darting toward a racked rod with the speed of a striking cobra.

Eventually, the day dawns when the kid's lure reaches a sighted fish before anyone else aboard can complete a presentation. No longer a kid by now, he is accepted as top rod, and his euphoria knows no bounds. But a lump fills his throat at the next meeting when his old tutor offers him a toast, and with misty eyes says, "You know it's going to happen someday . . . that somebody is going to come along who's faster than you are. But that doesn't make it any easier to take."

Even at that proud moment, while every elbow in the club tilts upward to honor his ascension, a chill creeps over the young man's spine, for he suddenly realizes that somewhere on a windswept seawall or a lonely canal bank there stands, this very night, an unknown but dedicated lad who is whipping the water to a froth as he trains for the inevitable day when he will step out of nowhere to take his own turn at challenging the Fastest Rod in the Gulf Stream.

Chicken—King of Flavors

I first heard it said about froglegs when I was but a rosy-cheeked lad. "Froglegs," some adult sage was forever commenting, "taste just like chicken."

There was a time, too, when I had not yet sampled

alligator meat. I wondered aloud about its taste. "Tastes like chicken," I was told.

As a college student in Tallahassee, I often fished the nearby Gulf Coast. One day out of Carrabelle, I caught my first cobia. So self-important did I feel about its gigantic size (15 pounds, as contrasted to the one- or two-pound trout I was then catching on my luckier days) that only as an afterthought did I ask the man at the fishhouse if my catch was good to eat.

"You kidding?" he said. "That's the best fish there is. Doesn't even taste like fish. Tastes like chicken."

And many a time I've heard that quail, pheasant or partridge tastes like chicken—as well they should, being cast in the same biological mold.

And then I read a newspaper wire-service feature that described a booming eel business on the St. Johns River.

"They look like snakes," said the story. "They sell like hotcakes," said the story. "They taste like . . ."

You guessed it. Chicken.

Now fresh froglegs, if you can find any in gourmet markets, are likely to sell for $10 a pound. Cobia fillets wear tags reading six or seven. And alligator meat also hangs somewhere up there where you don't get much change, if any, from a sawbuck. A single pen-raised quail costs three to five dollars, and other gamebirds are proportionately priced.

As to the value of eels, the aforementioned newspaper piece reported that they sell for as much as $15 a pound.

Something escapes me in all this. Why would any

one fork over up to $15 a pound for alligator, frog, cobia, quail or eel in order to get the taste of chicken when the real thing can be purchased for less than a dollar a pound?

For the price of a single frogleg dinner at your neighborhood French restaurant, you could probably eat for a week at Colonel Sanders. And the taste would be the same—or so "they" say.

The truth is, of course, that chicken actually tastes like none of the above. In fact, it does not even taste much like chicken any more. Soused liberally with a secret blend of 11 herbs and spices and blanketed in a golden crust, the total product may be pretty savory, but the chicken underneath all that is a flavorless product—the result of sterile cooping and vitamin-antibiotic chickenfeed.

If somebody made me the offer, I would be tempted to trade some froglegs or cobia for a good old-fashioned yard pullet.

If I had any eels I'd trade them for a lot less than that.

The Truth Will Out— And Then Some

Herb Allen, *Florida Sportsman's* regional editor in West Central Florida, is also outdoor editor of the *Tampa Tribune*, and in leading off one of his *Tribune* columns he noted that there are several ways to write a fishing story.

"As a last resort," he said, "you may even decide to write it truthfully." He added that he had "decided to opt for the latter course."

Now Herb has been a pal of mine for many years and I thought I had come to know him pretty well. But I had no inkling he was considering such a drastic change in style. Nevertheless, I am delighted that he took such pains to emphasize the truthfulness of the story that followed, which occupied two successive columns in the *Tribune* and which dealt with a writers' fishing tournament in which we had both participated.

Lest Herb think I am trying to give him the needle, let me admit right off that he beat me in the tournament—a fact which he reported truthfully, although immodestly. Again, however, I wish to emphasize his newfound regard for the truth.

Herb also truthfully reported that a fishing resort in the Keys had gathered together a dozen of the nation's finest fishermen— these being angling editors and writers from various Florida publications, along with a couple from such outposts as New York and Chicago.

At the end of a day offshore, I returned with a raft of points and a dolphin that turned out to be the biggest fish of the day.

Sad to say—but truthful—Herb had a few more

points than I did. We finished one-two in the competition.

It was a bitter pill for me to swallow, but I took solace in remembering the time when Herb and I staged a two-man angling duel in which I finished second while he finished next to last.

But back to the Keys tournament. Herb took the championship trophy and truthfully reported that I was runner-up.

I also received a trophy for my bull dolphin, the largest fish caught in the contest. Herb reported this fact too, and before I quote him let me remind you just once more that he had sworn himself to the truth at the very beginning of his coverage.

"Dunaway's 170-pound dolphin," Herb wrote right there in the *Tampa Tribune*, "proved to be the heaviest fish."

I had thought the dockside scale read 17 pounds when my dolphin was hung up. Obviously, these old eyes had deceived me.

Some unkind souls might suggest that the weight reported in the paper was a typographical error—a gremlin to which no publication is immune.

But as far as I'm concerned, my dolphin weighed 170 pounds, and if you don't believe it you can take it up with Honest Herb.

Herb Allen later retired from the newspaper without ever retracting the officially announced weight of my gigantic dolphin. The International Game Fish Association, however, was not convinced and still lists a puny 87-pounder as the world record.

Test Your Mental Morbidity

I use a question-and-answer column from time to time and would offer them more often but for the inconvenience suffered, for months afterward, of dodging all those university presidents pressing to heap honorary doctorates upon this modest head. At any rate, readers are invited to test their own meager knowledge against that of our skilled staff of outdoor writers. Score yourself as follows: 0 correct—normal; 1-2 correct—borderline idiot; 3-4 correct—permanent psychotic; 5 or 6 correct—expert angler.

* * * * * * * *

Q—I haven't fished for very long, but one thing I do know from seeing pictures of Huckleberry Finn is that you must use a cork or float. Trouble is, I have tried every float on the market and can't keep any of them atop the water. Some go under almost as soon as I put them out. Others stay afloat longer, but finally they too begin to tremble and dance. Then—kerplunk! Under they go. Am I doing something wrong, or are all bobbers defective?

A—Chances are you have made the common mistake of putting bait on your hook. Leave off the bait and the floats should ride high and dry indefinitely.

* * * * * * * *

Q—I have been told that crabs catch the most permit. Is this true?

A—Possibly. But their dispositions generally improve once the permit is in the net.

150

* * * * * * * *

Q—No matter where I fish on the coast—flats or channel, bridge or boat—the only thing I catch is catfish. Do you have any suggestions?

A—Afraid not. Fishing writers never catch catfish, although we do land quite a few whiskered trout.

* * * * * * * *

Q—I have been reading ads about a computerized fishing reel that can be button-programmed to let line out to a certain depth, bring it in and, in general, do everything the fisherman used to do to a reel manually. Is this the ultimate reel technology?

A—No. A reel is now on the drawing board which will go fishing all alone, permitting you to sleep late on Saturday morning.

* * * * * * * *

Q—I do a lot of fishing for seatrout. As you know, these must be 12 inches long to qualify as keepers. My problem is that I can never remember to take along a tape measure when I go fishing. Can you suggest some common object that could be used to measure my trout?

A—A foot-long hot dog works perfectly.

* * * * * * * *

Q—Having thumbed through a copy of Florida Sportsman at the barber shop, my husband got all excited and decided to take up fishing. I cannot afford to outfit him all at once but his birthday is coming up and I would at least like to buy him a fisherman's three most basic needs. Please tell me what they are.

A—Beer, insect repellent and Vienna sausage.

Where Rivers
Have No Names

One raw and wintry day of long ago I stood shivering on a dock, awaiting the arrival of the guide who was scheduled to take me fishing in mangrove country of the Gulf Coast. I wished he would hurry, for I was sure he was going to cancel the outing and permit me to sneak back under the warm blankets in my motel room. Instead, he showed up wearing three flannel shirts, two jackets and a broad grin of anticipation.

"Perfect day!" he bubbled. "We're really gonna get 'em!"

There are said to be 10,000 islands in that corner of Florida. I was new to the country then, and I would have sworn under oath that the count was conservative. Certainly we must have wended our way among many more than that before finally coming to a frozen halt far up a remote coastal river.

As promised by the guide, we really got 'em. On virtually every cast we hooked our bucktails into the jaw of a snook or redfish—unless perchance a ladyfish or baby tarpon grabbed it on the way down.

My excitement was exceeded only by my naivete when, during a coffee break, I breathlessly asked, "What's the name of this river?"

There was a long moment of silence as the guide put down his Thermos bottle and stared bleakly toward heaven, no doubt mulling over the possibility that his answer would appear in Florida's largest newspaper, for which I wrote a fishing column at the time.

At last he answered:

"This river ain't got no name."

Years later, the guide confessed to me what I had always suspected. The river had a name after all. He should have told me its name when I asked, he said. He just couldn't bring himself to do it because of fears that my column would send everyone in South Florida pushing and shoving those long and tortured miles through the maze of mangroves to his cherished river. He had been ashamed of himself ever since for not telling me, he said.

"Well, then," I asked. "What *was* the name of that river?"

"It's been so long now," he replied, "that I forgot."

This should indicate how difficult it is to get in the last word with an Everglades-country native. I don't recall that I ever did, and I doubt that Charlie Waterman ever did either, even though he is a master at wordplay.

But I am happy to note that Charlie keeps trying, in the material he writes for *Florida Sportsman* and in various books about his personal adventures, particularly those involving the old mangrove philosopher, Ted Smallwood. I eagerly hunt down and gobble up Waterman's tales about Everglades City, Chokoloskee, the Tamiami Trail and the assorted characters who roamed there in those heady days of not-so-long-ago before the National Park Service put up so many markers that canoeing visitors from Podunk could boldly go where no man had gone before. No man, that is, except Smallwood and the native fishermen he typifies, and Waterman and the back-country angling adventurers *he* typifies.

There is only one character who is central to all of Waterman's Ten Thousand Islands stories, that being Charlie Waterman himself. When it comes time to count characters, Charlie is not only a skilled counter, but a most deserving countee.

Defining the Aquapleasure Quotient

One aspect of the recent controversy in regard to commercial fishing on Lake Okeechobee, and its effect, good or bad, on the speckled perch population, has not yet been mentioned by biologists or fully taken into account by fishermen.

And it may remain a mystery until some enterprising independent researcher acquires a government grant to study and report on (as expressed in typical biological language):

"The Aquapleasure Quotient of Lunkerstrings as

compared to Limitstrings When Defined in Terms of Recreational Canepole-Days on Lake Okeechobee."

The study is needed because, if the planned management program works out in textbook fashion, then it is illogical to expect that masses of fishermen ever again will string their limits of speckled perch (crappie) day after day—as they have done in some of the good seasons past.

Instead—and we're still talking about textbook results only—anglers will catch a lot fewer fish but should bag about the same poundage.

The principle of fish management at work here is that a given body of water can support just so many pounds of perch. If the species becomes over-populated then stunting of individual fish results. Anglers may catch a lot of fish but they are all peanut-size.

This is what the biologists tell us has happened on Okeechobee. Anglers find it relatively easy to land a limit of 50 perch but they average, at best, a half-pound.

In a well-balanced lake, specks can average nearly a pound, with two-pounders not uncommon.

Thus, one aim of the plan to allow commercial fishing is to reduce the speck population, bring it into balance and produce larger and healthier fish. Opponents say that commercial fishing will kill the fishery entirely, but that debate is not the subject of this little piece.

Getting back to the textbook, let's over-simpli-fy and say that the fellow who used to catch a string of 50 fish weighing 25 pounds will, in the future, still catch 25 pounds but only 25 fish.

The obvious question now is: Will this fellow be as happy as he was before? It will take a long study of aquapleasure values to tell for sure.

Conclusions will be elusive, and the researcher will have his work cut out for him. Suppose he finds, say, that an eight-ounce perch takes 3.2 aquaseconds to land, but that a 16-ounce perch does not double the fighting time, contributing only 4.7 Canepole-Seconds of Aquapleasure. That statistic would seem to favor a larger haul of smaller fish. But there are other important factors to consider. Fishstringing-Hours and Scalescraping-Eternities might well swing the balance back toward fewer but larger fish.

The final judgment may be determined by the all-powerful influence of the Meat-Pound. A single fish will certainly turn out more edible ounces of flesh than will two fish half its size.

Besides that, when you eat one husky panfish instead of two skinny ones, you are bound to spend fewer Bonepicking-Minutes per Fisheating-Hour.

Pop Out Your Popeil

"The greatest improvement in fishing since the artificial lure" is now among us. Perhaps you have seen the advertisement that carries those very words. It refers to a baitcasting reel seat designed so that the line goes under a built-in bridge and follows the guides along the underside of the rod, as in spinning.

"New and revolutionary," says the ad, pointing out that this design gives your fishing rod a lower center of gravity, which, as we all know from reading about sports cars, is much to be desired.

But new it isn't. Certainly there must be a few other greybearded anglers around who can recall a similar rash of advertising that hit the fishing magazines in the late 1940s. I amaze even myself by recalling that this earlier underslung arrangement was named, aptly enough, the Underslung Fishing Rod.

Sad to say, the Underslung Fishing Rod soon went under, but a better fate may await its revolutionary revival. The Underslung, you see, was introduced at the very same time that spinning tackle began to boom. Baitcasting and all its components were being placed on the endangered species list by many pundits. Now, of course, that kind of tackle teems once more, and so if the greatest invention in fishing since the artifical lure doesn't make it, it won't be for lack of interest in baitcasting.

And if it does succeed, maybe someone should go back to the same era that produced the Underslung and revive another revolutionary product of those post-war years—the Stubcaster.

The Stubcaster was made of spring steel. In fact, it was actually a steel spring. It went into a coil just forward of the full-size baitcasting reel seat, and had an overall shaft length of about 18 inches. Because of the coil spring, said the ads, it could cast as far as the five- and six-foot steel and bamboo rods then in vogue.

But talk about bad timing. Not only did spinning tackle come along to steal the Stubcaster's thunder, but so did fiberglass rod blanks.

We sure had fancy fishing gadgets in those days. Being a nostalgia freak, I'm happy to see some of them come back. Not only is there a reincarnation of the Underslung, but also a device which works vaguely on the principle of the Stubcaster. I'm referring, as you've guessed by now, to the Popeil Pocket Fisherman.

Obviously, the Popeil is a much more elaborate mechanism than the Stubcaster. It has its own built-in spincast reel. It folds up (sometimes when you want it to). It comes equipped with hook, line and bobber. But still it features a stubby little rod that works (if that's the word for it) by spring action.

Some laugh at the Popeil but its day of acceptance in serious fishing ranks may be close at hand. We have found room for other light-tackle specialties, such as spinning and baitcasting, so why not for pocketing?

Eventually the International Game Fish Association may be compelled by sheer numbers to establish a world record category for pocketing. The records will not be kept by line-test, but according to quick-draw time—total time elapsed between whipping out one's Popeil and landing a pinfish, stumpknocker or whatever else the device may prove capable of catching.

Angling inventiveness isn't dead yet. Once more we cry: "Why didn't I think of that?"

The bright future foreseen by their inventors for "the greatest angling invention since the artifical lure" and for the Popeil Pocket Fishermen did not come to pass. Interest in the reel seat fell off (along with the seats themselves, no doubt), and all the Popeils disintegrated—most of them in the middle of a cast.

Introducing the New Angling Awards

A new look is creeping into the traditional lineup of fishing awards. More and more tournaments are beginning to offer trophies for a variety of different achievements, and not just for bringing in the most or largest fish.

We can applaud this trend for several reasons. For one, it helps remove the emphasis from sheer killing of fish. And it helps anglers appreciate the simple fact that fishing offers many satisfying experiences besides that of catching a monster.

From the tournament's point of view, a wide variety of awards is bound to attract more participants and more trophy sponsors. But, of course, there is the problem of thinking up feats that merit recognition.

In the spirit of public service, I have come up with a few ideas for trophies which I offer free of charge to any interested tournament. The suggestions even include ideal sponsors.

How about these?

The Old Spice Trophy for Most Ladyfish Caught.

The Greasy Kid Stuff Trophy for Most Ladyfish Released.

The One-A-Day Vitamin Trophy for Most Enthusiastic Deep-Jigger.

The No-Doz Trophy for Most Active Night Fisherman.

The Charles Atlas Trophy for Strongest Hook-Set by a Bass Fisherman.

The National Enquirer Trophy for Tallest Fish Tale.

The Tasco Binocular Trophy for Sailfish Released the Longest Distance from the Boat.

The Wisk Trophy for the Cleanest Fishing Shirt (wife's award).

The Right Guard Deodorant Trophy for Oldest Chum Used.

The Exxon Trophy for Bass Boat with Most Horsepower.

The Valium Trophy for Largest Moray Eel Caught by a Woman.

The Curity Bandage Trophy for Largest Catfish Stomped by an Angler Wearing Tennis Shoes.

The Morticians Association Trophy for Bridge

Fisherman Most Stubbornly Refusing to Use Catwalks.

The Seaquarium Trophy for Angler Catching Largest Shark.

The JAWS Trophy for Shark Catching Largest Angler.

The Ben-Gay Trophy for Most Amberjack Fought on One Trip.

The Pepto-Bismol Trophy for Most Vienna Sausages Consumed on One Trip.

And the top award:

The Tourist Council Trophy for Visiting Angler Making the Most Casts at Leaping Mullet.

A Survey of Random Interests

A random sampling of angling interests in the Greater Miami area (possibly the most random ever taken anywhere) has certainly turned up a wealth of random information. Analyzing it, I fear, is beyond the capability of this corner, and so I am merely passing it on for whatever random interest it may hold.

Among the polled portion of the populace, I found it rather intriguing that more than 300 referred to themselves as "Fisher," while only six used the term "Fisherman." Fifteen prefer to be called "Hooker," and 21 like to be addressed as "Rodman." Fourteen consider themselves a "Skipper," but 30 are content to be called "Seaman."

In fishing specialties, a great many random interests were represented. As opposed to the seafaring types at the end of the preceding paragraph, only one person says he is a "Wader." Among the other angling categories are "Popper," 19, "Spinner," 13, "Spooner," 10, "Netter," nine, "Caster," eight and "Troll," three.

It should come as no surprise that a large and random variety of fish species was named, or that the most popular one was "Bass," 133.

The others, in descending order of prominence, were "Pike," 34, "Salmon," 32, "Fish," 20, "Marlin," 19, "Jack," 18, "Bone," eight, "Carp," eight, "Snook," four, "Pickerill," three, "Drum," three and "Bream," two. "Perch," "Gar," "Trout," "Cuda," "Tuna," "Bonito" and "Sail" appear only once in the listings.

Perhaps you never realized that Salmon, Pike and Carp are to be found in South Florida, but I assure you they are. The source is irrefutable.

And, incidentally, there is only one "Lunker."

On now to preferences in bait. "Herring," believe it or not, was far ahead, being named 45 times. This compares to only four mentions for "Shiner," three for "Bunker," three for "Mullett," four for "Crabb," two each for "Worm" and "Chubb," and one for "Pilchard."

Tackle, Accessories and Rigging also occur at random in the sampling. Again, the statistical value is difficult to assess, but the tabulation shows 17 "Hooks," six "Hook," 11 "Creel," 11 "Leader," 13 "Knott," five "Rod," two "Reel," three "Spool," three "Lines," two "Line" and three "Cork."

Although this area is famous worldwide as a saltwater fishing center, you would never know it from the survey, in which various fresh waters were listed far more often than any sort of salty fishing environment.

I must emphasize that this information is taken straight from printed reference material and so there can be no mistake, regardless of how strange it might seem that "Rivers," appears 46 times, "Lake," 32 times, "Eddy," 14 times, "Pond," seven times, "Pool," nine times, "Hole," four times, "Cove," three times, and "Channel," "Creek," and "Sea," once apiece.

If you insist on verification of the foregoing random information you may check the white pages of the telephone book. All the words in quotation marks are listed there as residents of Greater Miami.

The Threatened Return Of the Rose Bowl

J ust a few short years back, early-morning anglers cruising a couple of miles offshore from Miami

Beach were often treated to a magnificent sight, and always in the same spot.

Silhouetted black against the rosy sky of a new dawn soared dozens, perhaps hundreds of seabirds —gulls and terns in all their streamlined splendor, hovering, darting, diving continually to the surface.

If this was your first sighting of the spectacle, your heart would leap to your throat and your hand would press mercilessly on the throttle, imploring your tired old engine to deliver rpm it never owned. Perhaps you didn't have much angling experience back then, but you at least knew that such an immense flock of excited seabirds could signify nothing but a ravenous school of gamefish.

Well, almost nothing, you soon found out.

You may have first suspected that something was amiss when you noticed that other boats in the area, some much closer to the birds, were not racing you to the scene. In fact, they were heading away from it with increasing speed. But you powered on, goaded even more by the frantic screams of the birds that now were close enough to be heard over the roar of your engine.

Finally you arrived within casting distance, and though the light still wasn't too good, you spotted a huge brown boil under the birds. Your trembling hand cut the throttle and reached for a fishing rod. What a giant school of fish *that* must be!

About then, the first errant breeze of the still morning wafted across the calm sea, passing over the brown boil on its way to your innocent and unsuspecting nostrils. Your first thought was that a

Russian submarine had unleashed a cloud of poisonous gas. As if the wake of a supertanker had struck your boat, you staggered across the deck, gasping. Blinded, desperate, you groped for the throttle and spun the wheel, and at the last possible second before losing consciousness, you gratefully gulped down long draughts of upwind air.

You had blundered upon the infamous "Rose Bowl"—an outfall depositing Miami Beach's untreated sewage into the Atlantic Ocean.

The Rose Bowl passed into the realm of nostalgia when Miami Beach tied up with Dade County's sewage treatment system. Now, nostalgia may once again turn to nausea, for we learn that the Miami Beach City Council is threatening to pull away from the county and once again start dumping the city's raw sewage into the sea. Such a move would seem to be illegal under state law, but remember that laws can be changed, and that many politicians view environmental laws as little more than targets to be shot at.

If Miami Beach *should* manage to accomplish the smelly project, then similar outfalls would likely become the rage among municipalities all along the Florida coast, inasmuch as this kind of sewage disposal is far cheaper than any other—in budgetary terms, that is.

The new Rose Bowl, they say, would be in deeper water than the old one—about 300 feet. The vastness of the ocean, we are assured, would assimilate the human waste as effectively as it does the waste from the countless marine organisms that abide therein and have no sanitary facilities of their own. But would it? Remember, many human beings produce unbelievably large amounts of such waste, prominent among them being those politicians at every level of government who always seem to be groping for new ways to pollute our waters. They're full of it.

Hey, Sports, Let's Share the Load!

Thanks to the miracle of dredge-and-fill, Floridians have for many years been able to watch the growth of gleaming edifices atop what used to be mere marshes and estuaries inhabited solely by the lower life forms.

Modern machinery was also introduced long ago to our interior woodlands and wetlands. Dredges and bulldozers were put to work draining this, razing that, filling the other, straightening out our untidily crooked streams and throwing up imposing barriers to keep fresh water from running off and being wasted in some ecologically sensitive but agriculturally useless coastal swamp.

Such once-unbridled spurts of progress have been controlled somewhat better in recent years, but outdoorsmen continue to lose vast chunks of recreational land to sheer population spread. For instance, my own house now sits in a suburban development that replaced what was once my favorite dove field.

Am I the only one who realizes that rank discrimination is at work here against fishermen and hunters? Why must we be the only recreational interests called upon to sacrifice our playgrounds to the cause of progress? Golfers and tennis players and, yes, even sports spectators should be called upon to share the burden.

But did you ever hear of a shopping center being built on the fairway of a golf course? Or tennis courts being lined over for parking spaces? Or agricultural runoff being backpumped into municipal swimming pools?

It's too late to hope for equal treatment, but it's high time we started trying to reverse the sad situation. I have a couple of ideas.

There must be six or more major football fields in Florida. For a good geographic spread we could take three of them—say the Orange Bowl, Gator Bowl and Tampa Stadium—and build a high-rise condominium in the center of each. Dimensions would be about 60 yards by 120 yards by 100 stories. The stadia could be left standing and converted into multi-level parking areas around the condos—a splendid touch, and the major ramps are already in place.

Fair is fair. We appreciate the fact that the Corps of Engineers generally leaves a roadside park or two on each of its hand-carved waterways. In the same spirit, we would roof the new condos with athletic turf so that football still could be played, even though would be viewable only on television.

Additionally, half the horse and dog tracks in Fl

da should be selected (by random drawing) for conversion into water impoundments. Since they already have high fences it would be nothing for the Corps to bulldoze earth against the fences to create levees. Rain would fill the new impoundments quickly in an average summer, and fish would be stocked in them. Naturally, there would be cycles of low water and of high. During low water years many fish would die. Too bad, but it happens. In flood years, the horses and greyhounds would huddle on a few meager islands of spoil left in the infield of each track for just such a contingency. They might suffer a bit from crowding and dampness, but they could survive on bales of hay and sacks of Dog Chow dropped by helicopter.

A Record Number
Of Records

It used to be that holding a world record would give an angler bragging rights—at least among his own pals. He could even come out second best on the day's catch and still shortstop the inevitable gloating of his buddy by casually re-dropping the well-worn information that he was the holder of a *world record*.

The statement would be delivered in a bored tone that fairly dripped with the implication that the holder of a *world record* does not lower himself to such childish rivalries as seeing who can yank the most snappers into a boat.

But things have changed drastically in recent years. The International Game Fish Association—now that it has taken over freshwater records, added many new species worldwide, plunged into flycasting, and tacked on several line-test categories as low as two-pound—currently lists several thousand records and possible records.

Not counting ties.

Even the IGFA itself cannot tell you exactly how many record niches there are, because they will now accept all-tackle record applications for virtually *any* species of fish anywhere in the world.

And of the officially listed niches, hundreds are as yet unfilled.

All of which means that a fisherman no longer has much justification for bragging about a world record. Quite the contrary. Any angler worthy of the name who cannot lay claim to a world record nowadays must have a terrible inferiority complex. There are two obvious routes to a cure: either undergo long-term therapy or get out there and fill at least one of those vacant niches in the IGFA record book.

The latter course would seem to be the easier, if the more expensive. Flyrod records alone contain such inviting targets as black marlin on two- and four-pound tippet, swordfish and white shark in all tippet classes, and numerous inviting vacant records for such prizes as smallmouth buffalo, brown bullhead, burbot and several species of gar.

Land any one of them and your inferiority complex should melt away like paint on a plastic worm.

Strangely, however, many anglers maintain that not even all those thousands of IGFA records are enough to do justice to the truly great accomplishments in angling. This complaining faction holds that there should be a list of record *fishing* achievements, not just *catching* achievements.

They fret over the lack of a Guiness-like book of angling records in which to record such historic feats as the world's largest backlash, or the longest string of four-letter words uttered in one breath by a fisherman trying to start a balky motor.

It happens that each of those records has a claimant, but for the lack of an official sanctioning body, their deeds must remain unofficial.

The most four-letter epithets are said to have been mumbled by the captain of a 25-foot, center-console, tuna-towered, twin-engine fishing machine as he was being towed to port by two teenagers in a rubber raft. The count was 912, representing 11 languages.

As for the world-record backlash—described as resembling seven sheep dogs fighting over a mop head—it occurred when a surfcaster neglected to check clearance for his backcast and consequently stuck two sets of treble hooks into the ear of a passing policeman. Simultaneously, as fate would have it, a deerfly chose that very moment to sink its choppers into the ball of the angler's casting thumb, so that he momentarily lost all thought of thumbing the spool.

So huge was the backlash that the angler could not pick it free, even though society granted him 30 solitary days in which to try.

Where Was NOAA When The Reefs Went Out?

All our lives we are asked to ponder the imponderable: "What happens when an irresistible force meets an immovable object?" "Which came first, the chicken or the egg?" "Is there life after death?"

And now South Florida sportsmen have been set to chewing on a new one:

"Were there deep reefs before NOAA?"

NOAA, as you may know, stands for National Oceanic and Atmospheric Administration. It is an arm of the U.S. Department of Commerce, and itself has many arms. I will not ask if one arm knows what the other is doing, as it is apparent that some of them barely know what they are doing themselves.

It is an arm of NOAA, for instance, which tells us that the seas are going to be, "three feet or less." Only when we arrive at the offshore fishing grounds do we discover that they mean three or less than Mount Everest. Another branch of NOAA makes discoveries, one of which—headlined on page one of Florida's largest newspaper—was the discovery that the coral reefs in the Upper Keys do not dead-end at the line of surface visibility after all, but keep right on going out there into deep water, as deep as 100 feet or more; even 200 feet.

Discoverers operate with a lot more flair than they did in 1492. NOAA almost immediately took a U.S.

171

senator down in a mini-submarine to verify the new discovery. Columbus never took Queen Isabela to the New World. With one discovery under its belt, NOAA may now be encouraged to even greater heights, possibly even to the discovery that the water in Biscayne Bay extends all the way from the surface to the bottom, or that the range of opossums is not limited to backyard garbage cans but extends well out into the woods. Watch for these developments on page one of Florida's largest newspaper. Most of the countless anglers who have been drawing fathometer pictures of NOAA's newly discovered reefs for many years, and who have been plucking grouper and other fish from them since even before depth sounders came into use, do not particularly mind the fact that their old stomping grounds are now documented as a discovery in the archives of NOAA. Neither do the many scuba divers, who have been enjoying those reefs for nearly as long. But a handful of sportfishing captains do mind. NOAA, you see, also blabbed the fact that there are a number of uncharted wrecks out there, noting that some of them are wooden and so perhaps date back to the time of the Spanish Main. Actually, they date back to about the Miami River derelict period, when they were salvaged by the aforementioned skippers and furtively sunk as private fishing holes. NOAA at least is keeping the exact locations of the wrecks secret, fearing exploitation by treasure seekers. This makes the captains feel a little better, since the treasure involved is in the form of fish fillets—more precious than gold these days—and in the scrap-lead value of deep-jigs and heavy sinkers.

Problems? Try a Boat, Wife and Kids

The ocean is a pretty big place, stretching off to infinity in nearly every direction. Anyone who is out there trying to troll up a few fish must constantly ponder the problems of which direction to troll in, and for how long. One reader wrote to brag that in his family, those problems have been solved.

"We had been skipping ballyhoo in a southward direction about four miles due east of Fowey Light off Key Biscayne, when my wife abruptly informed me that she had by then received too much sun on her left side and that I would have to run the boat in the opposite direction for about an hour and a half in order to even her up.

"I feebly tried to explain that our trolling speed was barely overcoming a fast-flowing Gulf Stream, which is why we had been managing to stay in the same general area. But she won the point. When the time came to quit fishing—that is, when her tan had evened up—we found ourselves far north, off Hollywood, facing a long run back to Key Biscayne."

The missing information in this tale, obviously, is how many fish were caught, if any. But that certainly isn't as important as a balanced tan. Regardless, this seems as good a system as any for deciding which way to troll, and is certainly much better than the usual system, if for no other reason than that you don't lose any coins over the side while flipping them.

Sadly, though, deciding on a trolling route was not the only problem besetting our reader. In addition to a boat and wife, he has a dog and two small boys. Idle flattery, perhaps, but he says they all enjoy *Florida Sportsman*, although the dog, admittedly, tried it only once and ate only half of it then.

The wife we have heard about. Since she is not in a position to defend herself, we will go on to the boys.

"Our mail is delivered in mid-morning [Editor's Note: He must live inside a post office]. By the time I get home from work, the boys (ages five and three) have examined my copy of the magazine from cover to cover. Most of the fishing pictures have already been torn or scissored out and taped to their wall or into their coloring books."

This reader is not always so unlucky, however. For example, it was his good fortune to be selected among the one-in-every-thirty subscribers who were privileged to spend some of their valuable free time filling out a *Florida Sportsman* questionnaire. One question asked what kind of things readers would like to see more of, and less of, in the magazine.

"I'd like to see more," he responded "of myself resting in my easy chair, reading your magazine and fantasizing that I was the angler doing battle with the blue marlin.

"I'd like to see less of my tribe beating me to the magazine. Perhaps you could include an editorial warning that the ink will cause a lady's fingernails to crack, and that kids who perform

surgery on *Florida Sportsman* will get warts."
Hey, kids, he's not kidding. Don't blame the
toads.

Food for the Thoughtful Angler

*As the reader will note momentarily, this column
appeared at Christmas time.*

Following is a compendium of observations
and philosophical tidbits too short to become columns of their own, but each so thrilling, provocative,
insightful, learned or instructional that none could
be held in the file any longer—not without a new
bottle of air freshener, anyway.

—The man who spends a great deal of his time
fishing in salt water, and a great deal more of his
time fishing in fresh water is known, of course, as a
bifishual. A recent survey discloses that bifishuals
are at highest risk of suffering from the dread condi-
tion AIDS—Acutely Imminent Divorce Suit.

—Christmas gift suggestion: the angler on your
list already owns all the computerized pH meters,
color selectors, lure selectors, depth sounders and
fishing reels listed in the mail order catalogs.
But don't despair. He still needs a gigantic multi-
compartmented tackle box in which to carry the va-

rious batteries, attachments, inserts, accessories, fuses, tools and instruction pamphlets necessary to operate his electronic anti-fish strike force.

—In light of the above, let us pause and consider that fishermen used to sit around the dock and argue the effectiveness of the Zara Spook against the Chugger, or the Rapala against the Rebel. Now they sit around the air-conditioned marina bar and debate the merits of the Eveready compared to the Duracell.

—A recent news item reported that the harvest of codfish has declined sharply in New England. This could mean that a lot of Florida restaurants will run short of fried grouper.

—Confusion has arisen over the use of the word "pole," which has two meanings in angling terminology. One is the kind of pole you tie a line to and fish with. The other is called a "pushpole" because guides push it deeply into the mud to hold the boat while they wait for fish to blunder within casting range.

—Fishermen find a variety of uses for toy balloons, They make handy marker buoys and excellent fishing floats. Best of all, they can be filled with water and heaved at the nitwits who anchor in your chum line.

—Next time you travel north in the winter you're sure to see, in many backyards, cordwood piled up like snook.

—When you cast along a mangrove shoreline or woody stream bank it really isn't necessary to keep throwing your plug into the branches the way you've been doing. Cast it into the water instead. If you find fish in the branches, you won't have to cast for them; you can paddle over and pick them like oranges.

—When I once expressed horror at a grizzled old angler (GOA) for fishing with a rusty hook, he asked: "Who cares if the fish gets lockjaw?" Today, I would snappishly retort that every responsible sportsman *should* care. He should keep his hooks meticulously sharp and clean, and maybe even sport a bumper sticker saying, "Help Stamp Out Piscine Tetanus."

—I know it's Christmas season already, but I forgot to warn you in October that Halloween is the night when banshees return from the grave, screaming like reel drags.

Do We Need a Bounty on Snook?

A furtive informant who identifies himself only as "Deep Trout" and who purports to be a confidant of Fuller Bulschid, the powerful state senator from Kumquat County, has relayed some disconcerting reports concerning the senator's growing impatience with the problems caused by the ups and downs of snook in Florida in recent years.

According to Mr. Trout, Sen. Bulschid is preparing a bill which will place a bounty of five dollars on each snook taken in the state, the aim being to eliminate the snook from Florida waters.

"Think of the headaches this will cure," the senator is quoted as saying. "No more hassling over closed months and bag limits. No more endless biological studies, symposia, intensified law enforcement, fish hatcheries and similar drains on the state treasury."

I hasten to point out that my inverview with Deep Trout took place—at his insistence—after dark on a lonely mangrove islet, and that no documentation was offered. But the minnow bucket that Deep Trout wore over his head imparted to his voice a sepulchral, echoing tone that made one's hair stand on end and begged one's serious attention.

To my protest that the anglers of Florida would not stand idly by and see the snook eliminated, he cut loose with a guffaw that would have lifted the bucket from his head but for the plastic bail under his chin.

"As the senator said," Deep Trout said, "an angler's interest in fish is surpassed only by his interest in money—as witness the unending stampede to participate in cash-prize tournaments and the rush to fishhouses at the end of the day by anglers bearing Saltwater Products Licenses and coolers of fish to sell.

"If the senator were proposing to *poison* all the snook he'd be lynched. But by proposing to have the state *pay* for every one that's killed he expects to be acclaimed a hero and probably elected governor."

The informant further noted that Sen. Bulschid considers the snook a dangerous animal and feels

178

that its elimination will save Florida citizens much pain and suffering. He bases this belief on his own chronic back problem, which began last summer when he was carrying his catch of 13 large snook off the dock of his vacation cottage on the West Coast. And only a month ago, one of the many nieces who frequently accompany him to the cabin suffered an agonizing muscle strain while attempting to follow the senator's instructions on how to gig a snook.

"Two severe injuries at one small dock," the senator is said to have said, "can be extended into a massive safety hazard statewide."

Our talk continued into the wee hours. Deep Trout explained that provisions of the legislative bill will require anglers to send their snook, gutted and frozen, directly to Sen. Bulschid in order to collect the $5 bounty. There will be an obvious waste problem, so to avoid having piles of rotting snook besmirching the landscape and polluting the air, the senator has personally volunteered to handle the disposal of the frozen carcasses. This he will do by air-shipping them to Japan for disposal there.

His bounty program, the senator believes, may prove valuable in the management of other species as well—notably, trout, redfish and king mackerel. The bounty might later be expanded to accommodate those and other species, depending on how efficiently the disposal system in Japan operates.

For my part, I nourish the hope that much of the above is unfounded, or at least exaggerated. Still I wish to state my emphatic opposition to a bounty on snook, regardless of the amount paid.

Odd Questions, Odd Answers

Most of the detailed angling instructions in *Florida Sportsman* are handled either in Angler's Clinic or in feature stories. But odd questions keep coming in that can't be conveniently dealt with elsewhere, so we have saved them up and will attempt to dispose of them here.

Q—On the left side of my baitcasting reel there is a dial with some numbers. What is its function?

A—The dial is called a backlash control and is used to control the size of your backlashes. Set the dial on "2" and you get a two-snarl backlash, on "4" a four-snarl tangle, and so on.

Q—Just forward of the foregrip on my flyrod is a tiny guide in the shape of a "U". Since this "U" is at right angles to the rest of the guides, I'm wondering: Am I supposed to thread my line through it?

A—Don't bother. That isn't a guide at all but a hook-keeper—so called because it keeps hooking your flyline at inopportune moments.

Q—What is an egg sinker?

A—These questions are supposed to be about fishing, but I'll answer anyway. An egg sinker is used to sink eggs to the bottom of the the pot so that they will boil evenly.

Q—I have heard my grandfather refer to a metal ferrule. Do you know what he's talking about?

A—In your grandfather's day, a metal-to-metal ferrule was used to permanently convert a two-piece rod into a one-piece rod. In recent years it has been replaced by a glass-to-glass or graphite-to-graphite ferrule, which converts a one-piece rod into a two-piece—generally when you deliver an energetic cast.

Q—Two questions: (1) Has anyone invented a ballyhoo rig that doesn't require making a leader pin and wrapping with copper wire? (2) If so, does it work?

A—(1) A lot of people have. (2) They all work, but not as hard as the fishermen who rig their ballyhoo with them.

Q—How do you keep a grouper from going into a hole?

A—The same way you keep a snook from going into the roots.

Q—I've noticed that on nearly all spinning reels the handle can be converted from the left side to the right? Why is this?

A—This allows you to crank a spinning reel with your right hand without having to turn it upside down.

Q—What is the difference between a graphite rod and a boron rod?

A—On average, 50 or 100 bucks.

Q—Is there really something called a curved butt that's found in the cockpit of an offshore fishing boat?

A—Yes, but it is more often found on the sundeck of a sailboat.

It's Raining Revolutionary Revelations

Angling technology continues to advance so rapidly that no one seems able to stay abreast of even the everyday revolutionary inventions.

As this is being written, I am but two weeks returned from the nation's largest fishing tackle trade show, which featured more than 1,300 different display booths.

Fat chance of seeing anything else revolutionary, I have been telling myself ever since, yet right here on my desk, barely a fortnight later, sit several press releases describing ideas that somehow managed to elude all of the great tackle minds represented at the show.

First there is the "Dinner Bell Spin," which, according to the news release, is "a fishing lure that incorporates a series of bells and other special devices to attract fish."

Leaving nothing to chance, the very same lure also "provides a series of hooks attached to the frame which can be baited for additional attraction."

A stroke of genius! Bells and other devices and baited hooks too, all in one irresistible offering! But you certainly must be asking yourself where in the world you could acquire enough bait to keep a whole series of hooks appetizingly adorned.

By a great stroke of luck, another press release bears the solution, telling of a "portable (thank God!) device for finding and collecting worms."

Aptly named the "Worm Grabber," this machine "features a set of rollers powered by a small battery-operated motor assembly which grasp the worm and deposit it in a tubular collection chamber." No mention is made of whether the worms reach the collection cylinder in a whole state, or if perhaps they must afterward be squeezed from the tube like toothpaste.

Anyway, once you get your bait, the challenge arises as to how you might affix all these bells, other devices and series of baited hooks to your line. An obvious answer is the "Compensator Leader," which "enables the fisherman to better control the action of the rod, hook and line when playing a fish that has taken the hook."

Ingeniously, "the device attaches to the line above the hook with swivel snap fastening to achieve maximum flexibility and movement."

But, alas, it turns out that all these lovely revolutionary items are but carrots dangled to tease us. The tantalizing information is offered only as "human interest" material. "Functional or constructional details" were deliberately withheld from the press releases. Industrial spies, one must suppose, are everywhere.

But here's something you can rush out and buy even now "at most fishing tackle stores and sporting goods outlets where fishermen's needs are sold." It's a "revolutionary (of course) scented Fishbait Mix" that can be prepared (are you ready?) *right in your own microwave oven, in the privacy of your own home* .

Privacy, no doubt, will be virtually guaranteed as soon as you open the oven door.

Offshore Angling Glossary

Sooner or later, the urge to travel offshore and do battle with giants of the sea strikes every saltwater angler. Be advised that this is not the kind of fishing that can be undertaken impulsively. There are many things to learn, of which rigging the baits and handling the tackle are but minor portions. Far more important, and more difficult, is reaching a full understanding of the talk, titles and terminology. Many subtleties are involved, but you should have no trouble if you carefully study the following definitions.

* * * * * * * *

BLUE WATER: Deep offshore water, typically dark blue in color, where the majority of big-game fishing is conducted.

GREEN WATER: The color to which blue water turns once the occupants of the offshore boat have finished hanging over the side in rough seas.

CAPTAIN: Supreme ruler of the ocean and all its

minions; a descendant of Poseidon, God of the Sea (see Flying Bridge).

FLYING BRIDGE: The seat of all knowledge, wisdom and power; the Mount Olympus of an offshore fishing boat (see Captain).

COCKPIT: The mortal world of toil and error, far below the Flying Bridge.

HEAD: A small room located belowdecks of a fishing cruiser in which the angler stations himself immediately prior to every strike.

KNOCKDOWN: The release of a fishing line from its outrigger pin. Also: the fate of an angler who tries to beat the mate to the rod after the line is released.

LINE DOWN!: The mate's cry which alerts the Captain on the Flying Bridge, the angler in the head and the guests hanging over the side that a knockdown has occurred.

FIGHTING CHAIR: A piece of furniture which, in combination with a giant fish, becomes an instrument of indescribable torture, surpassing in agony even the infamous Iron Maiden of medieval times. Used normally, it functions as a sunbathing platform.

PULLED THE HOOK: Phrase denoting that a fish has been lost in a manner that reflects no blame on angler or crew. Often expressed in southern Florida and Latin America as, "No my fault!"

BROKE THE LINE: Phrase denoting that a fish has been lost through fumble-fisted incompetence on the part of the angler or Captain, depending on which is speaking.

185

RAISED A FISH: Phrase indicating that a fish was sighted following one of the baits and laughing at it.

WOULDN'T EAT: Phrase expressing surprise at the reluctance of oceanic gamefishes to include plastic, metal or the carrion remains of long-dead baitfish in their diets.

BACKING DOWN: A three-way contest in which the boat, running backward, tries to overtake a fish, running forward, before the angler, running in circles, can become involved.

A Fish By Any Other Name

One man's fluke is another man's flounder, but that's only because the two men do their fishing in different places.

Although regional variations in fish names are legion, they cause little confusion among knowledgeable anglers, who eventually absorb many of them through reading or travel. Anyone who doesn't recognize a flounder (Florida style) as a fluke probably has caught so little that he thinks it's a fluke when he catches anything at all.

The challenge of identification gets far trickier when the names of the fish are changed deliberately and for studied reasons. Commercial fishermen do this all the time, in hopes that a coined name will hide the true identity of whatever disgustingly ugly creature it is that they are trying to put on your table.

Unfortunately, they are not very good at the renaming game. While they figured, quite correctly, that it would be difficult to shove something called a goosefish down our throats, even if we did not bother to look up a picture of one in the dictionary and faint dead away, they goofed royally in the new name—calling this aquatic apparition a "monkfish."

And when New Zealand started shipping over a fish that in the Atlantic is referred to as a "slimehead," the same flair for promotion was put to use in rechristening it the "orange roughy."

I suppose more restaurant-goers will have the nerve to order monkfish and orange roughy than goosefish and slimehead—but not many. Actually, both those fish are very good but you still have to coax them onto someone's plate.

Where the commercials make their big mistake is in not consulting the sportfishing sector. Renaming fish in order to improve their image is old hat to anglers, and the names they come up with are virtual paragons of euphemism, guaranteed to remove even the faintest traces of stigma from the most lightly regarded of catches.

For instance, headboat fishermen in Florida will tell you that porgies do not frequent local waters, their ecological niche being filled here (as the crew will readily attest) by the similar but much more prestigious "silver snapper."

Those strange, bewhiskered fishes common everywhere along the Florida coast are not really catfish, as you may have heard them called by the uninformed, but the far sportier "three-spined trout." A closely related species is the "bearded bass." The "spiny tailed flounder," however, belongs to a different family.

Offshore charterboat fishermen often think they are fighting the rare "brown marlin," only to find upon leading the quarry to boatside that they have caught a shark instead.

Florida inshore light-tackle fishermen can tell you glowing tales about their encounters with the "hardtailed pompano," a coveted gamefish that hits like a ton of bricks and fights like a miniature submarine.

And all along the Gulf Coast, anglers brag about the fabled "saber-toothed snook," a gamester readily identifiable not only by its prominent dentition but by its black-tipped fins.

There are plenty more irresistible names where those came from. So next time, you commercial guys, just ask. But I'm afraid it's already too late to do much about the monkfish.

The Basser's
Secret Language

An anthropological study undertaken by an obscure but distinguished southern university has proposed the startling theory that bass fishermen may not, after all, be illiterate.

An interim report from the study hints that the public perception of bassing illiteracy is based largely on the observation that bass fishermen cannot spell the simple three-letter word "hog," instead rendering it as "hawg."

Though cautioning that their findings to date must be classed as preliminary, the researchers suggest that "hawg" may not be a misspelling at all, but the key word in a highly complex language developed by bass fishermen to mask the inherent frustrations of their chosen pursuit. The study may one day prove that bassers, far from being illiterate, are able to communicate among themselves in words that are jibberish to anyone else, with the possible exception of porpoises.

The report further claims to have decoded a

few words of the bassing language and lists them as follows:

HAWG: The basic word of a bass fisherman's vocabulary. It does not refer to a domestic swine or the fisherman himself, as many believe, but to any bass of grossly disproportionate abdominal dimension, hence the confusion.

GROUNDHAWG: A hawg that has been prepared for food by running through a meatgrinder, it being unsuited to any form of culinary preparation other than the making of fishcakes, and of doubtful edibility even there.

DAWG: A pet kept by bass fishermen, chiefly for the purpose of disposing of the aforementioned fishcakes.

KELLAWGS: The cereal eaten for supper by a bass fisherman after he has sampled the fishcakes and given them to his dawg.

FRAWG: A noisy amphibious creature said to be a premier bait for hawgs.

BAWG: The habitat of a frawg, composed in equal parts of earth, water and noxious vegetation.

SLAWG: To walk wetly through a bawg.

FAWG: A dense atmospheric mist associated with bawgs. The bass fisherman who slawgs through fawgy bawgs pursuing frawgs deserves to catch a hawg. He usually catches pneumonia.

GRAWG: A bracing hot rum drink frequently taken by bass fisherman after they are rescued from fawgy bawgs.

NAWG: A similar drink to grawg, but made with eggs.

TAWGS: Clothing worn by bass fishermen, consisting primarily of jumpsuits of sickly color adorned with embroidered patches.

LAWG: The lurking place of a hawg. Also, a record book kept by a bass fisherman in which he carefully notes the month, day, hour, minute, second, moon phase, wind, cloud conditions, water depth, water clarity, water temperature, air temperature, pH level, dissolved oxygen, barometric pressure, the activity of cows in nearby fields and the various other scientific factors that are responsible for his not catching anything.